8 SIMPLE **BUSINESS WRITING** TIPS

BOOKS IN THE 8 SIMPLE TIPS SERIES

8 SIMPLE BUSINESS WRITING TIPS

8 SIMPLE TIPS TO MANAGE UP

8 SIMPLE **BUSINESS WRITING** TIPS

HOW TO WRITE WITH PURPOSE, CLARITY, AND CONFIDENCE AT WORK

JAMES DARE

PUBLISHED BY
PUDDING LANE PRESS

Cartoons by Ersin Ertuk

Published by Pudding Lane Press
Third Edition 2023

ISBN 978-0-6456687-1-1

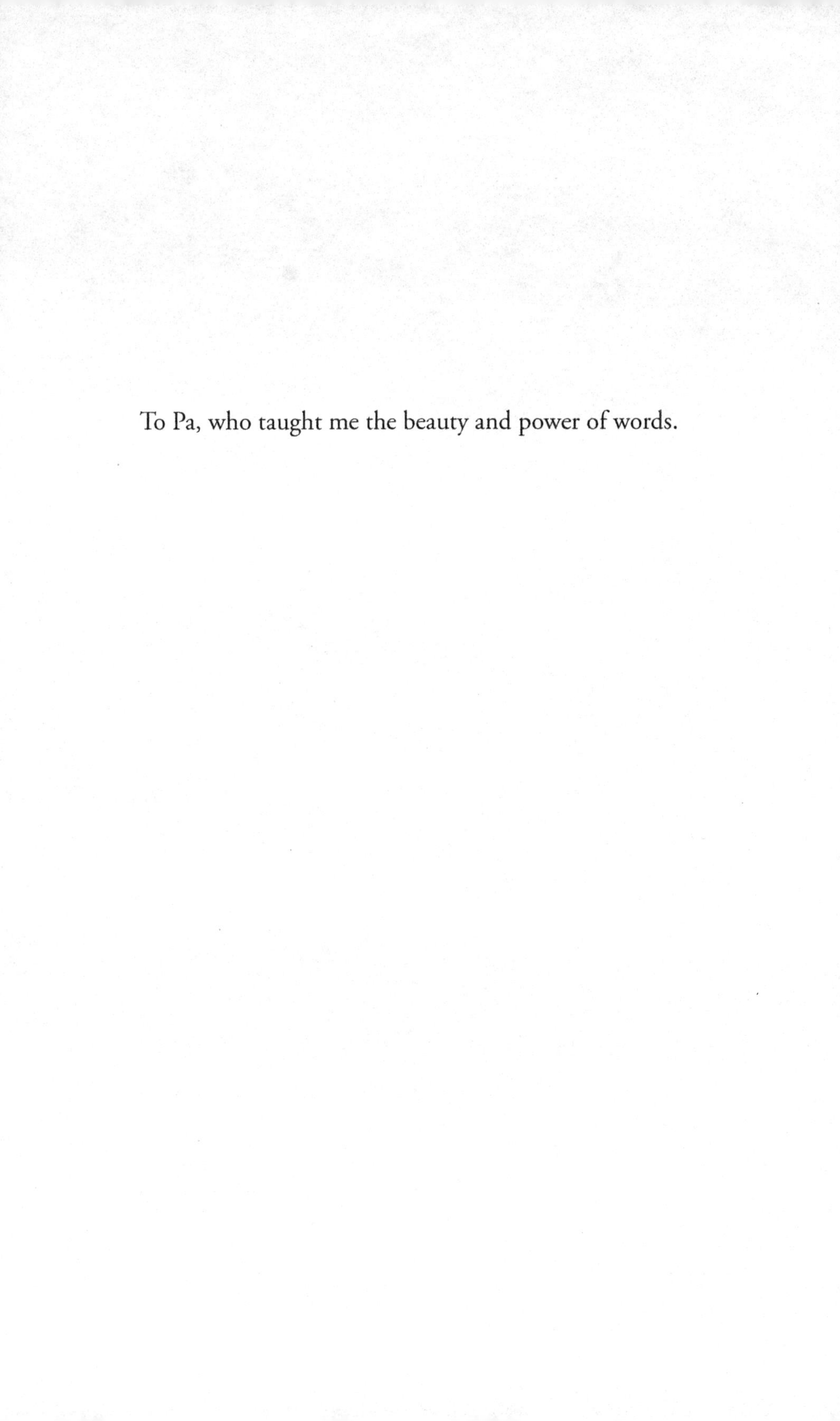

To Pa, who taught me the beauty and power of words.

Table of Contents

Introduction

The scariest moment is always just before you start.
After that, things can only get better. –Stephen King

Tell me if this scenario sounds familiar. Your boss has asked you to write a presentation for a new client. You sit at your desk, staring at a blank screen, desperately willing the right words to magically appear. As the hours pass, the looming deadline adds to your panic. You need to write something, anything.

In desperation, you type the first thing that comes to mind, resorting to jargon and technical terms, hoping to impress your reader. However, the end result resembles a chaotic mess of jumbled sentences rather than the masterpiece you envisioned.

Trust me; we've all been there.

Now, imagine a different scenario. Picture yourself as a confident business writer, able to express your thoughts clearly and purposefully. When you circulate your finished document, you do so knowing that your words will engage, persuade, and inspire action. Your colleagues appreciate your work, your boss nods in approval, and your client is happy.

Sounds like a better scenario, right? Well, I have good news for you. Business writing is a skill that anyone can learn.

Good business writing is not about using fancy words or merely ensuring correct spelling and grammar. It's about connecting with your readers, understanding their needs, and crafting compelling messages that resonate with them. It's about presenting information that is easily understood, leaving no room for misinterpretation, and making a lasting impact on your audience.

As a business communication professional, I've been helping individuals, businesses, and brands tell their stories for over 25 years. I've witnessed the power of effective business writing firsthand, helping to influence decisions, build trust, and drive results.

Based on my experience, I've developed eight simple tried-and-tested tips to help anyone who wants to improve their business writing. Whether you're just starting your career or are a professional looking to refresh your skills, I want to help you make communicating at work less daunting.

So, if you're tired of wasting time on ineffective communication and are ready to take your business writing to the next level, you've come to the right place.

Why Good Business Writing Matters

In today's fast-paced world, time is a precious commodity. Few have the patience or inclination to decipher long-winded emails or convoluted reports. Research shows that people in business spend more than 25 hours per week reading, and 81% say poorly written content is a massive time-waster (Bernoff, 2016). The last thing you'd want is for your reader to feel like they've wasted their precious time reading a document you wrote.

As you hone your business writing skills using the tips in this book, you'll start to see the benefits that good business writing can have. You'll spend less time deleting, rewriting, and editing your content, freeing you up to focus on more important tasks. You'll gain more influence as your readers begin to see the value you can provide. What's more, your readers will know precisely what actions you want them to take after reading your document. Over time, your confidence will increase as you see the impact your good business writing is having.

Conversely, mediocre writing is not merely a missed opportunity; it's a liability. Poorly crafted emails, confusing reports, and incomplete proposals reflect poorly on your abilities and on your organization's reputation. There may even be legal implications for your company if you don't research properly before you start writing. The stakes are high, so it's essential that you get it right.

How to Use This Book

What sets this book apart from others on the subject is that it's not merely a collection of grammar rules or templates for business correspondence. Instead, it's a guide that's simple and easy to follow that will improve how you communicate at work.

The first eight chapters each focus on a different tip for successful business writing. Followed in order, they outline an approach to business writing, starting with defining why you're writing, understanding who your reader is, and structuring the messages you want to deliver. We'll then explore how to make your writing inclusive and accessible—critical in today's modern world—formatting for maximum readability and editing your work to avoid embarrassing typos, punctuation, spelling, and grammar mistakes. A cheat sheet is included at the end of each chapter to summarize the key takeaways and act as a handy guide you can refer back to.

As you read the tips, I encourage you to use what you learn. You don't need to wait until the end to improve your writing.

Later in the book, we'll look at some best practice examples you can use when you put these tips into practice, as well as handy online tools, resources, and checklists to help you make your business writing as easy and effective as possible.

Get ready to transform your writing, enhance your professional presence, and achieve the results you desire. It's time to unlock the power of good business writing and propel yourself and your organization towards success. Let's get started.

Tip 1:
Define the Purpose of Your Writing

Definiteness of purpose is the starting point of all achievement.
–W. Clement Stone

In this chapter, you will learn

- why it is important to know why you're writing.
- how to define the purpose of your writing.
- the different types of business communication.
- when to use written communication … and when not to.

Have you ever sat for hours writing what you thought was an acceptable report on the project you're working on, only to realize later that you've missed the point altogether? Do you ever feel defeated by your struggle to get your message across? Or do you frequently spend more time explaining what you were trying to say than you can fit into your busy schedule?

This is where my first tip to help you communicate better at work comes in: You need to know why you're writing. In short, before you can start writing, you need to define the purpose of your written work. What impact do you want to make? What lessons do you want your reader to gain from your written work? What actions do you want your readers to take? Spending a few minutes thinking about your purpose is a crucial first step in effective business writing.

The Importance of Knowing Why You're Writing

The purpose of your writing forms the foundation of your written content. As such, it's critical you get this right. The purpose of your writing relates directly to what you hope to achieve through your written communication. If you don't define your purpose correctly, you could be communicating the wrong message, and your attempts at communication might fail.

Let's look at an example. Say you're working on a project, and your manager requests a progress report. You spend hours making sure all the small details of the project's progress are included. Yes, some managers will want this—we will discuss this in more detail in Tip 2—but the majority only actually want three questions answered:

- Will you make your deadline?
- If not, why not?
- Is there anything you're struggling with and can't solve by yourself?

Now, you've gone from thinking you need to send your manager a detailed report to discovering that all they want to know is if everything is on track. Therefore, the purpose of your communication is to reassure your manager, not provide them with every single detail of what's happening.

Business writing is rarely done without a good reason and expecting specific results. Having clarity on the purpose of your writing can help you determine who you need to communicate to, what messages will add the greatest value to the reader, and what action you want to drive as a result of your writing.

How to Define the Purpose of Your Communication

Sometimes it can be obvious what the purpose of your writing is. When it's not, I've found the *Five Whys* approach highly effective. To do this, start with what you think your purpose might be and ask yourself "why" five times to work your way back to the true purpose of your communication. Let's take promoting a new soft drink as an example:

- **Initial purpose:** Promote the new soft drink.
- **First why?** So that my customers know about it.
- **Second why?** So that they understand it's the superior product on the market.
- **Third why?** So that they will want to try it.
- **Fourth why?** So that they will realize they need it.
- **Fifth why?** So that they buy it.

You've now gone from thinking that your purpose is to promote a new soft drink (inform) to realizing that the actual purpose of your communication is to make a sale (persuade). Knowing this information will help you determine what to include in your writing and how to structure your message, which we'll discuss in Tip 3.

Keep in mind that you don't have to ask "why" five times. Ask as many times as you need until you are sure you know what the purpose of your writing is.

You should be able to write your purpose in a simple sentence, such as: My purpose is to _____ so my reader will _____. For example, *My purpose is to inform staff of a new ordering process so that my reader will understand the new steps they have to follow and be able to implement them.* When you eventually write your content, always refer back to your purpose. This will help you stay on track and increase the chances of your writing achieving the desired outcomes.

Different Types of Business Communications

The purpose of your written communication will help you determine the business writing approach you should take. Let's look at the different types of business communication, when you would use each, and what you should include:

- **Instructional.** This type of communication tells the reader what steps they should take to complete a task or produce a specific outcome. It is a directional style of writing that is often used for user manuals, action plans, and when introducing new processes and methods for completing specific activities. Instructional writing should be clear and precise, and easy to follow. Steps readers should follow should be listed in chronological order.

- **Informative.** This type of business communication is used where specific information is recorded. Many business documents fall into this category, including meeting minutes, business reports, and financial statements. Informative communication will often include detail and statistics. Include the facts and avoid superfluous information.
- **Persuasive.** When you are trying to impress the reader and convince them to buy your product or invest in your business, you will use persuasive communication. It is usually used for marketing documents, sales pitches, or when proposing a solution that will need endorsement. In this type of writing, you will include all the relevant information about your product, service, or company to influence the reader's decision. You can use more emotive language and stories to communicate your message. Don't fall into the trap of listing all the features without explaining how they will benefit the reader or end user. Your reader will ask, "What's in it for me?" so make sure you tell them.
- **Transactional.** This type of communication usually refers to communications that relate to the exchange of money, goods, services, or credit. It includes quotes, invoices, and forms the reader may have to complete. Only include information required to complete the task.

When to Use Written Communication ... and When Not To

Once you've determined your purpose, it's good practice to ask yourself if written communication is the most effective way to achieve it. Written communication is ideal when you have to convey important messages, decisions, and instructions and when you need to keep proof of the communication. It can also be the ideal method when the person you need to communicate with is at a different location or when either person involved in the communication will need to refer back to what was said in the future. Let's look at specific instances where written communication can be preferred:

- **Conveying detailed information.** If you have to discuss a complex topic and are concerned that some details may be lost in other forms of communication, written communication can be ideal. You can then ensure that all the necessary details are included in your communication and that your readers can refer to them whenever they need to.
- **Need a permanent record.** If you need to keep proof of your communication, it can be best to keep it written. Retaining a record is particularly important when tracking compliance, addressing workplace problems, or recording decisions that may need to be referred to and used as evidence in the future.
- **Talking to a large audience.** When you need to send a message to a large audience and it will take too long or won't be possible to speak to everyone involved, it can be helpful to put it in writing and then send out a bulk email.
- **Avoid interaction.** Sometimes you may need to convey a difficult message that you know won't be well received by your audience. Using written communication can help to avoid interaction with others in these situations.
- **Require a uniform application.** If you are introducing a new process and want different people to apply it in their daily work, it can be best to put it in writing. This way, you can make sure everyone receives the same message and can then follow the process in the same way.

Sometimes other forms of communication, such as verbal communication, can be better than putting it in writing. Some of these instances can include the following:

- during crises when there's no time to write a letter or email
- when the message may be misunderstood in writing
- to brainstorm and share ideas

- to get clarification on something
- when a personal discussion can get the idea across successfully
- to resolve conflict
- to get instant feedback
- to avoid liability

To illustrate this point, let me tell you a story. Early in my career, I received an email from a senior manager. In it, he expressed his displeasure at some aspects of a project I was leading. In my opinion, he'd clearly been given the wrong information. I immediately hit "Reply" and started typing furiously. For each issue he raised, I wrote a detailed response. I drafted and redrafted, trying to strike the right balance between diplomacy and setting the record straight. Finally, after several attempts, I decided to get a second opinion. I forwarded the email to my boss and asked, "Do you think this sounds okay?" His advice came back in four simple words: "Pick up the phone."

What did I think my email was going to achieve? Initially, my intent was to clear my name and show that I was competently running the project. But, on reflection, I realized that my real goal was to rebuild trust so I could continue to have a productive working relationship with this person.

If you ever write something and you don't think it's going to be received well by your reader, stop and consider whether you'll be more likely to achieve your purpose by using another form of communication.

Tip 1 Cheat Sheet

The first tip for successful business writing is to know why you're writing. Your purpose is the foundation on which your communication is built. Here are some questions you can ask yourself to help define your purpose:

- Why am I writing?
- What outcome do I hope to achieve?
- What action do I want my reader to take as a result of my writing?
- Am I writing to instruct, inform, persuade, or transact?
- Can I use the *Five Whys* approach to help define my purpose?
- Can I put my purpose in a sentence? My purpose is to ____ so my reader will ____.
- Is written communication the most effective way to achieve my purpose?

Once you know the purpose of your written communication, you can move to the next tip: Know your reader.

Tip 2:
Know Your Reader

To make our communications more effective, we need to shift our thinking from "What information do I need to convey?" to "What questions do I want my audience to ask?"
–Chris Heath

In this chapter, you will learn

- why it is important to determine who your reader is.
- how to identify your target reader and their communication preferences.
- how to make your message relevant and useful.
- how to ensure a positive reaction to your writing.

No matter how good the message in your written communication may be, your message can get lost entirely if you don't keep your reader in mind while writing. Think about a time you received an email or letter full of technical language you didn't understand. You may have tossed it without even attempting to read it. Or, you might have received a letter that appeared to be written for elementary school pupils. You stopped reading it as you felt insulted by its extremely basic information.

The last thing you want is for the writing you spent hours rereading and perfecting to be deleted or thrown away simply because your reader couldn't identify with it.

This means that sometimes you might have to change your writing style to suit your reader and their preferences. For example, if your reader wants to receive information in a certain way or prefers to be communicated with formally instead of informally, you should adjust your writing accordingly. This might seem overwhelming initially, but as you improve as a business writer, adapting your writing style will become easier.

Considering who your reader is will determine what you say, how you say it, and even when you say it.

How to Identify Your Reader

Sometimes, it will be obvious who your reader is, for example, when you type an email or letter to a specific recipient. In other instances, it's crucial you spend some time considering who your target reader is so you can write your communication with this reader and their needs in mind. You need to ensure your written content answers all your readers' questions, making them more likely to accept your information. Knowing your reader will also help you anticipate their reaction to your content; if it is negative, you can prepare accordingly.

Let's look at some questions you can ask yourself before you start writing to help you determine who your reader is and how you may have to adapt your writing style to suit them:

- **Who is my reader?** This can be a known individual, a group of specific people, or even an audience you don't know. If it's a known individual or group of specific people, it is easier to determine what they would want from your writing. However, if your intended reader is unknown, it can be more difficult to alter your message accordingly. This can be the case if you need to write a report for senior managers you've never met before. Think about the type of reader you would like to attract to your writing, what they would expect in your content, and possibly just as importantly, what they don't want to see.

- **Is my reader an expert in the field?** If your reader is an expert, they may feel insulted if you don't use technical language. Conversely, if your reader is not an expert, you may lose their interest by including too much jargon. Again, this may be easier to determine if you are writing for a specific reader. If you're writing for an unknown group, consider who you would like your reader to be and how much technical language your ideal reader would like.

- **What level of seniority do they have?** How you will word a document for an intern at work will vastly differ from how the CEO at your company will prefer a report to read. Don't insult your CEO by writing content intended for the intern; similarly, don't confuse the intern with content meant for the CEO. However, regardless of who your reader is, be careful not to fall into the trap of using big and unnatural-sounding words. We'll discuss the importance of using plain language in Tip 4.

- **What do their age, demographics, or cultural background tell you?** These factors can have a significant impact on the type of information your reader will expect from your content. Considering these factors about your reader can also help you avoid offending them with your writing. If this sounds too overwhelming, don't worry; we'll cover how to be inclusive in your writing in Tip 5.

- **What do they already know?** This is another important question you should pay special attention to. Knowing what your reader may already be aware of can help to avoid boring them with unnecessary information. Conversely, if you leave out information that your reader is unfamiliar with but needs to know, your message may be misunderstood.

- **How much time does my reader have to read my content?** The CEOs and senior staff of most companies are busy and won't be able to spend too much time reading a report or email. Keep this in mind when you're writing. Most readers are lost after the first few paragraphs. If you don't make sure you get to the point quickly, your efforts at compiling your content may be wasted. In Tips 3 and 7, I will give you suggestions on how you can format your content for maximum effect.

- **Who might my secondary reader be?** Even if you are writing for a specific reader, always keep in mind that your content may be passed onto someone else. The email you send to your manager may be forwarded to their manager, or the finance department may also view the report intended for the marketing department. You shouldn't necessarily alter your writing just because there may be a secondary reader, but you should always remember this when you're writing, especially when it comes to issues of inclusivity.

The more you know about your reader, the better you can anticipate their needs and make sure you give them all the information they may need. Just because you may be overly familiar with certain concepts doesn't mean your reader will be.

How to Determine Your Reader's Communication Preferences

Another important aspect of understanding your reader is identifying their communication preferences. This is simply the way your reader prefers to be communicated with. Some people like lots of details, while others just want the bare facts. You might now wonder how you can tell who prefers what communication style. One way I like to do this is by considering personality types.

I've found the *Insights Discovery Profile Colors* a simple way to identify my readers and their needs (The Color Works, 2016). It works on the premise of four main personality types. If you wanted to study this in more detail, you could divide these four personalities into eight subtypes, but for this exercise, we'll focus only on the four main ones.

Fiery Red

These are the people who may appear to be highly competitive, demanding, determined, and sometimes even aggressive and impatient. They are extremely extroverted, have no problem asserting themselves, and often have high energy levels. They need to be in control at all times—which can almost seem dictator-like—and make decisions relatively quickly. These decisions are often pragmatic. They are very results-driven and can become exceptionally irritated by incompetency and indecision.

When you need to communicate with a Fiery Red, you can repeat the following mantra to yourself: *Be brief, be bright, be gone.*

- Don't make your communication with them too personal or use long intros. Instead, simply address them and get straight to the point. You will likely lose their interest when you make small talk in your communication.

- Get your point across to them quickly, don't bore them with too many details, and don't try to pad any bad news you may have to share. Show them what results you can bring in a very succinct manner.

- Be sure you've done your research properly, even though they probably won't want to see it. These people think quickly on their feet, and you need to be ready with answers. Make sure they will see the benefit of what you're suggesting.

Sunshine Yellow

If you have a co-worker who is always the life of the party, even on a typical day in the office, they likely fall in the Sunshine Yellow category. These people are as extroverted as they come. They thrive on being the center of attention and deeply want others to admire them. They are at their happiest when they can interact with others. Some of their deepest fears include others disapproving of them, and they generally don't like strict rules and routines. They make their decisions spontaneously and often based on feelings rather than facts.

When you need to communicate with a Sunshine Yellow, always remember that they thrive on entertainment, either entertaining others or being entertained.

- Always start your communication with them on a personal note. Grab their attention by showing that you care about them. This will make them feel valued, likely resulting in them continuing reading.

- Give examples of your suggestions or ideas, and if possible, use stories, colorful pictures, or infographics to help get the message across. People with this personality type may become bored with too much gray text.

- If you can, and the situation allows for it, don't be afraid to use humor in your communication. These people thrive on energy and happiness, so if you can help them feel good while reading your content, half your job of convincing them will be done.

- Whether you are selling a service or product, addressing a concern, or providing information, always focus on any aspect that might appear to be fun or interactive.

Earth Green

Have you ever looked at a co-worker—or even yourself—and thought that person is an extreme people pleaser? This person likely falls into the Earth Green category. These people are primarily introverted and care deeply for others, often to the point where they neglect their own needs to fulfill those of others. They also value taking care of the environment and often prefer green options, even if they cost more. They deeply want to be liked and keep the peace. Therefore, these people usually avoid confrontation at (almost) all costs. They take their time making decisions and want to consider all the information, including the pros and cons, in great detail. This can result in them often being indecisive and feeling overburdened.

When communicating with an Earth Green, remember to keep the information people-centered.

- Address them in a friendly manner, and if you know anything personal about them or their hobbies, feel free to ask them about this, such as, "How are your renovations at home going?"
- Give them a teaser of the purpose of the communication so they can have time to process what's about to be discussed before you hit them with the facts. For example, you can write something like, "You've come highly recommended in the field of gardening, and I would love to discuss a new natural pesticide with you."
- Then, focus first only on the benefits your product, suggestions, or ideas will have on people. Remember, these people will often place the interest of people above the bottom line, so you may lose their interest if you overload them with financial statements before addressing the advantages it will hold for people.
- Now, give them all the information they may need to make a decision. This will include information on your research, analysis, infographics, and financial statements or projections.

- End your communication by again focusing on the benefits your product, suggestion, or ideas will have on the people. Then, set a date that you will follow up after they've had time to review the information you've given them. Don't expect them to make a decision immediately, and try your best not to rush them. You may have to communicate with them frequently before they will make a decision. If you show an Earth Green that you're getting impatient with their indecisiveness, you might as well kiss the deal goodbye; these people typically thrive when others are patient and encouraging.

Cool Blue

When you think of an accountant, you might stereotype them as introverted, happy to avoid people by crunching the numbers all day and placing the business' bottom line above everything else. This stereotype is the typical Cool Blue. They are the rule followers who may appear to be formal and conservative. They thrive when they can solve problems and hate when others are careless or not as precise as them. They take making decisions very seriously and will need to have all the possible facts before opting for the most logical choice.

When you need to communicate with a Cool Blue, remember this mantra: *Give them all the details.*

- Greet the person formally without being personal. Don't ask them about their hobbies or family life. This will often result in them tossing your letter or deleting your email. Keep it professional.

- State the reason why you're communicating with them and what the potential benefits to the company may be. Remember, a Cool Blue person will care less about the impact decisions might have on the employees, so always stick to the benefits to the company. Tell them what proof you will include. This can help to entice them to read further, as they will know your potential benefits are based on logic and research.

- Next, give them all the information they will need. Even if you think certain information is unnecessary, it's best to include it. A person in this category will not make a decision until they're convinced they've received all the facts. Make your reports user-friendly by grouping specific information together, using links and subtitles. The typical Cool Blue will likely want to revisit particular details and check your facts or numbers, so make it as easy as possible for them to do this. Structure your document as logically as possible, and ensure you include solid facts; they thrive on logic and facts.

- Re-emphasize the impact your product, suggestions, or ideas may have on the business, and if you can, combine your statistics or analysis for them in a clear infographic. Don't worry too much about using pretty colors; they will likely look past them.

- If you've done your research well, provided all the facts, and structured your information clearly and logically, they may make a decision quickly after they've had time to consider all the information. Never get upset when a Cool Blue requests further information or research. In fact, you can see this as a good sign as they haven't rejected your proposal based on the initial facts provided.

- If they reject your product, ideas, or suggestions, don't argue with them unless you can present them with new facts and figures. Remember, they don't care how invested you might be in your proposal; if it doesn't make logical sense to them, you won't get their buy-in.

Take some time to observe how your colleagues interact in your business or organization. Are they Fiery Reds who want you to get to the point quickly or Cool Blues who love nothing more than diving into all the facts?

There may be times when you don't know your reader well enough to know their personality type or when you're writing for a group that will include many different types of people. This can make effective communication more difficult. In Tip 3, we'll explore how you can structure your writing to accommodate all four personality profiles.

Make Your Message Relevant and Useful

When it comes to the effectiveness of your content, there are two dimensions you should consider: relevance and usefulness. If your content seems outdated or poorly researched, it will lose relevance. And if it doesn't meet the needs of your target reader or if they can't see how your content can help them make decisions, reach their goals, or solve their problems, it will lose its usefulness.

To ensure your content is relevant and useful, take the time to consider what questions your reader will want you to answer in your writing. Since you don't have a crystal ball, it can be hard sometimes to know what all your readers will want to know.

If you have the opportunity, ask the reader. Too often, I've seen people write content that didn't hit the mark, only to find that if they'd taken a few minutes to ask the reader—or someone with insight into the reader—what they wanted to know, a whole lot of grief and second-guessing could've been spared. No one will think less of you for finding out what your reader wants to know. In my experience, senior managers appreciate people who ask questions and seek clarity.

If you don't have the opportunity to ask the reader or other colleagues, try doing some online research; for example, if you're trying to sell fertilizers, you can type "frequently asked questions on fertilizers" in the search bar. This will bring up the questions most often asked on your topic and may help you determine what you want to include in your writing.

After sending out a business report, you may get questions about it, sometimes even if answers to the questions are already in the report. It can be beneficial to make notes of the questions you're asked after sending the report, as this will give you a better idea of the aspects your reader would like more focus on. This will give you a head start when you need to write another report for the same or similar readers.

Always consider your content's relevance and usefulness to your target reader. Remember, what is useful and relevant to one reader, might not be viewed in the same way by another reader. Keep this in mind when you write.

Ensure a Positive Reaction

To ensure a positive reaction from your reader, it can be helpful to keep your writing reader-centered. By doing this, you're writing your message with your reader in mind, not necessarily the product you might be trying to sell. Let's look at ways you can achieve this in your writing:

- **Write for a person.** No matter what type of writing you're doing, always remember that a person will read it, not a computer. You are, therefore, not just relaying information through your written content but also building a connection and trust with your reader. If your reader feels respected, valued, or encouraged, they are more likely to respond positively to your writing. Refer back to the different types of personalities if you feel unsure of how you should communicate to your reader.

- **Address your reader.** If you're writing for a specific reader, as is usually the case when communicating via email, use your reader's name when you address them. This will add warmth to your email and show your reader you're talking to them, not at them, no matter how short the message may be. If you know the person well and know what they're interested in, what hobbies they have, or who their close family members are, you can consider asking the person about it, such as "How are the kids doing?" or "When was the last time you played a round of golf?" This personalized start to your communication can help to make your reader more accepting of your message. Remember not to include this personalized introduction if you're communicating with a Fiery Red or a Cool Blue.

- **Smile when you write.** When writing, you can't rely on your tone of voice or body language to help bring your message across. Therefore, you must write positively to invite your reader to understand and accept your message. One way of doing this is by smiling and imagining your recipient is sitting in front of you as you type. This might seem strange but give it a try the next time you need to communicate with someone in writing. You may be surprised by the response you receive.

- **Lose the first-person text.** If you try to avoid "I" language, particularly in your first paragraph, your reader will feel valued and more willing to continue reading. Change your "I" to "you" to address your reader directly. Instead of writing, "I believe you can help me with this," you can write, "You come highly recommended," or instead of, "I need your help," you can say, "You are the ideal person to help with this." It's a small change in how you construct the sentence, but it can make a big difference in how your reader interprets your message.

- **Be considerate.** Always respect your reader by considering the timing of your communication. Do you like it when someone asks you to complete an urgent report five minutes before the end of the workday or before you go on leave? Do you like to be copied on emails that don't involve you? Consider your reader before you send your written content to them.

- **Remember who your reader is.** This is often the main reason why your message may be misunderstood. Even if you've put a lot of thought into who your reader is before you start writing, it's important to constantly remind yourself of this as you're writing. As you get overly involved in your writing, you may lose focus on the reader.

- **Be clear in your explanations and solutions.** You may lose your reader's interest if your information isn't complete and precisely explained. Incomplete information and misunderstandings go hand in hand. Make sure you don't make this common mistake. Be thorough without being repetitive or boring. This skill can take some practice, but the more you write, the easier this will become.

- **Make sure you're inclusive.** Inclusivity means being sensitive to your reader's age, race, gender and sexual preference, cultural background, and beliefs, to name only a few. What might not seem offensive to you, may put someone else off completely. If you're ever in doubt, do an online search to make sure what you want to say doesn't have different meanings in other cultures or races. We will discuss this in more detail in Tip 5.
- **Logically organize your content.** Your reader will appreciate it if you take the time to structure your writing in a way that is easy for them to follow and understand. We will discuss this in more detail in Tips 3 and 7.

Tip 2 Cheat Sheet

When writing for business it is essential to keep your reader in mind. Your content may determine whether you get buy-in on your suggestions or make the sale. Let's recap the questions you can ask yourself to get to know your reader better:

- Who is my reader?
- Are they a known individual or group?
- Are they an expert in their field?
- What level of seniority do they have?
- What do their age, demographics, or cultural background tell me?
- What do they already know?
- How much time do they have to read my content?
- How does my reader prefer to be communicated with? What personality type do I think my reader has?
    - Fiery Red: Be brief, be bright, be gone.
    - Sunshine Yellow: Entertain them and keep the communication as personal as possible.
    - Earth Green: Focus on the impact my content will have on the people and/or the environment.
    - Cool Blue: Give them all the facts in a logical manner. Is my message relevant and useful to my reader?
- How can I make sure my reader reacts positively to my writing?

Once you're satisfied that you know the purpose of your writing and that you've taken the time to consider who your reader is, what their preferences are, and what they would expect to be included in your communication, you can go to the next tip: Organize your messages.

Tip 3:
Organize Your Messages

The reason business writing is horrible is that people are afraid. Afraid to say what they mean because they might be criticized for it. Afraid to be misunderstood, to be accused of saying what they didn't mean, because they might be criticized for it. –Seth Godin

In this chapter, you will learn

- how to define the messages of your written communication.
- different writing structures to consider to have the greatest impact.
- how to organize your messages and create an outline.

How often do you find yourself staring at a blank screen or sheet of paper, not knowing what to write or where to start? You might get frustrated, having put time and thought into the purpose of your communication and who you're writing for. But still, you can't seem to get started. You may even begin to feel anxious as the deadline for your report edges closer, and you still haven't written a single word.

This is likely because you still need to complete an important step in all forms of writing: organizing your messages. You may think doing this will take too much time and that your busy schedule won't allow this, but the more effectively you can organize your thoughts, the quicker you'll be able to complete your writing and deliver a well-planned and structured document to your reader.

Apart from this, you'll also save time when it comes to comebacks and questions on your written content, as you took the time to make sure everything that should be in your document is there in an organized manner. If nothing else, you'll surely impress the Cool Blues you communicate with.

The first steps in preparing your business writing are to define the purpose of your written communication and know who your reader is, as discussed in Tips 1 and 2. Now, you need to think about the messages you want to communicate and organize them in a way that will make sense to your reader.

How to Define Your Messages

When you take the time to carefully consider what you want to say and define the messages you want to send to your reader, your content will likely be much better understood and accepted. Defining your messages is particularly important when your document will have more than one message that you need to convey, and you want to make sure that you order them according to priority. Let's look at how you do this.

Do Your Research

Use the information you've gathered in Tips 1 and 2 to think about what further research you may have to do. Consider the questions your reader will want answered, and ensure you have all the information they need. The more research you do and know about your topic, the easier it will be to organize your thoughts. Look at what was included in similar reports or letters. Is this something you want to include in yours? What other information can you provide to your reader that's never been seen before? Allow yourself enough time to think about this and consider what information you have and may still need to provide your reader with compelling content.

Decide on Your Messages

Once you've completed your research, consider what the key messages in your writing should be. These are usually the aspects of your information that would be most interesting or compelling for your reader.

Your key messages will vary depending on the purpose of your document and whether you're writing to instruct, inform, persuade, or transact with your reader. For example, if your aim is to instruct your reader, your key messages would relate to the steps that need to be followed to implement the new process or achieve the required outcome. In persuasive business writing, the key messages are often the outcome of your research, a solution to a problem, or the biggest benefit your product can provide.

If there are multiple things you want to focus on, prioritize them in order of importance. The most important message is your primary message. Other messages are your secondary messages and should reinforce the primary message.

How to Structure Your Communication

Writing in a clear structure will help you get your message across, entice your reader to continue reading, and convince them to accept your offer or make a decision.

How you structure your written content will depend on the type of communication you're writing. For example, a sales pitch would be structured differently from an email telling staff about a new leadership appointment. A sales pitch would require detailed information as you're essentially asking your reader to leave the products they're familiar with to use yours instead. But, in an email informing staff of a new leadership appointment you can include only the details that apply including the name of the new leader, the role they've been appointed to, and when they start in the role.

Let's take a look at four structures commonly used in business writing.

The Pyramid Principle

The Pyramid Principle (Minto, 1978) is a structure for organizing and communicating information in a logical and concise manner. It's based on the premise that you lead with your most important message first. Here's how it works:

1. Identify the main message you want to convey to your reader.
2. Determine the secondary messages you want to communicate. These should be specific and reinforce the main message.
3. Order the secondary messages by importance.
4. Use specific examples and evidence to support each secondary message, making sure the evidence is relevant and convincing.

As you plot this information on a page, you'll see why it's called the Pyramid Principle.

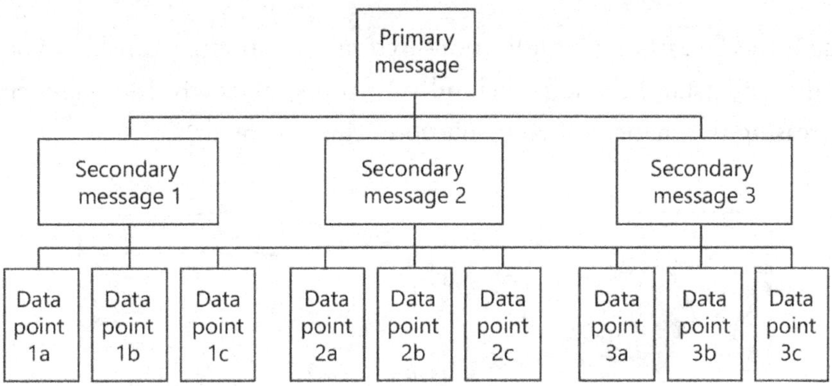

Figure 1: The Pyramid Principle

Using this structure can make your writing easy for your reader to follow and understand by providing a clear information hierarchy and reducing unnecessary detail. Readers who are time-poor or Fiery Reds will thank you for using this structure.

Later in this chapter, we'll work through an example that uses the Pyramid Principle structure.

Situation–Complication–Resolution

Another commonly used business writing structure is called Situation–Complication–Resolution. It can be very effective when communicating a problem and the proposed solution. You can structure your report or presentation under these three headings:

1. **Situation.** Describe the current state, including relevant background information about the problem or opportunity. This section establishes the context and need for the solution.

2. **Complication.** Describe what has changed to create the problem or opportunity. Include any constraints or challenges that need to be overcome.

3. **Resolution.** This is the proposed solution to address the problem or opportunity. This section should provide a clear path forward for your reader.

Using the Situation–Complication–Resolution structure can help your reader understand the logic behind your proposal clearly and concisely, increasing the chances of your solution being accepted.

Five Ws and the H

In the *Five Ws* and the *H* structure, your information is organized by Who, What, Where, When, Why, and How. Let's look at an example of how to write an email about a new process. You can structure your writing according to your answers to these questions:

1. **What is changing? How is it changing?** This is the information you should prioritize in your message.
2. **Why is it changing?** This will help the reader understand why this new process is necessary. If your reader understands the reason, you'll likely get their buy-in.
3. **Who is impacted?** This will help the reader understand whether they are directly involved in the new process.
4. **What do they need to do?** Explain to your reader exactly what they should do. This is your call to action.
5. **By when?** Give your reader the necessary deadlines for implementing the new process.
6. **Where can they get more information?** Let them know who they can contact or where they can find more information.

You can use all *Five Ws* and the *H* or just those that are relevant. When writing an email to communicate a business change, using this structure will go a long way to helping your reader understand the change, the impact it will have on them, and the actions they need to take.

The Three-Act Structure

Another way of structuring your writing was invented hundreds of years ago by the Greek philosopher Aristotle (Lanouette, 2012). His Three-Act Structure has been modified over the years to be used effectively in business writing of many different kinds, particularly when you need to communicate with those making the decisions. As the name suggests, this type of writing consists of three parts: the opening, the main body, and the close. It can be helpful when writing longer documents or proposals requiring a lot of information. Let's look at each of these three sections in more detail.

Opening

Unlike many other types of writing, this structure lets you open big with the conclusion. You start your communication by explaining why you're writing a report, a presentation, or a sales pitch. With the conclusion, you can also include some background in the Opening of your document. Try to keep your Opening to fewer than six sentences. The Opening isn't meant for long explanations—that is what the Main Body of your document is for. If you're writing for a Fiery Red, their decision will likely be based largely on your Opening, so make sure it's good.

Let's look at an example of how you may want to do this. For this exercise, let's say you're writing a report after your team investigated different ways to streamline production at an engineering plant. You can write something like, "Our team was asked to examine ways of streamlining production at ABC Engineering Works. After extensive research, we have developed four strategies that we strongly believe will make a big difference to the company's time and cost management. Our team concludes that the second option is the most favorable."

Your reader will know exactly what the report is about, that four potential strategies will be discussed, and that they should pay special attention to the second option. This opening will entice the reader to read further, as they will want to know what these four strategies are and how they can save the company money and time.

If you want, you can include another sentence or two in your Opening about the problem the report will solve. For example, "The cost of running an engineering plant has become increasingly high, particularly in the current financial climate. It has, therefore, become necessary to look at ways in which costs can be reduced by streamlining the production."

Adjust this further as your situation requires or according to your reader's preferences. As long as you get to the point quickly as to why they're reading the document and what your findings are, you should be good to go.

Main Body

In the Main Body of your document, you will provide all the details your reader may require. This is where you can give lengthy explanations and proof to justify your findings. If you're writing for a Cool Blue, most of their attention will be focused on this section, so make sure you make it worth their time.

This is also where you can shine by presenting the hard work you've put into your research and finding solutions for your reader or by giving them a product that can solve some of their problems. If you've done your work thoroughly, you have the right to be proud of what you're presenting to your reader. However, always keep the reader in mind and remember that the information you're giving them is not about you as the sender but about the reader and their needs.

Discuss the reader's problem in as much detail as you need to while keeping your reader's potential limitations in mind. Make your reader feel understood. Then, introduce your findings and make sure you include a solution for every problem they have on the specific topic.

Once you've declared your solution, offer potential alternatives. Show them the pros and cons of these alternatives, but remember to return to your solution or findings and why they are the superior choice.

Justify this by providing detailed analysis, statistics, financial forecasts, or financial statements if you have them. If you're concerned about the length of your document, you can include these in appendices. If you're working on an electronic document that won't be printed, you can link these using hypertext. We will discuss how to do this effectively in Tip 5.

When including your analysis, it can be helpful to prioritize it in order of importance and urgency. Your reader might only want to look at one or two points to make a decision, so don't expect them to rummage through pages of statistics and infographics. A general rule of thumb is to start with the more technical analysis and then move on to the non-technical statistics. This will depend on the type of industry you're in and the document you're writing.

Closing

End your document by referring back to the Opening. Explain briefly what was discussed in the document and describe how your approach, solutions, or product can help the reader through their pain points or problems. Keep this concise but include everything that you feel will make a difference.

If you need the reader to make a decision based on your document, such as approving your request, approach, or sale, be clear on what you require them to do and by when.

Close your document by explaining how your reader can direct any questions they may have and when you'll follow up with them.

If you want to be proactive, you can create a separate document where you answer questions you think your reader may have. You can link to this in your document for the reader's perusal. However, do keep in mind that most people won't actually read this separate document, but it can help you respond quickly to questions you may get if you've already compiled some answers.

Never get annoyed if a reader asks you a question that you know has been answered in the document. Some decision-makers will ask questions simply to be heard or to show you they're in charge. Answer these questions in as much detail as you can while staying calm.

How to Create an Outline

Once you have done your research, know what messages you want to communicate, and have determined the structure that will be most effective, the next step is to create an outline.

Let's work through a content outline example using the Pyramid Principle structure we discussed earlier.

Start by writing down the purpose of your communication—so you keep this top of mind as you write—followed by your primary and secondary messages.

Do this in whichever way works for you. You can jot them down on a sheet of paper, use tables in Microsoft Word or Google Docs, or enter them in Microsoft PowerPoint using a separate slide for each message. Don't worry about whether your messages are in logical order; you'll work on ordering them properly later.

For this exercise, we'll look at writing a sales presentation to sell digital advertising space on a popular website.

What is the purpose of my communication? (What outcome am I trying to achieve?) *To persuade the reader to buy advertising space.*
My primary message is: (This is where you explain to your reader why they should care about what you have to say. What's in it for them? Ensure this message is compelling and stands out.) *This advertising space will help the reader to grow their business.*
Possible secondary messages I might use: (These should reinforce the primary message.) • *Benefits of advertising on this website* • *Visitor traffic* • *Low cost* • *Proven results*

It's worth noting that you might be working with more or fewer secondary messages depending on the type of document you're compiling, the complexity of your messages, and your reader's communication preferences.

Continue to build the outline by adding supporting facts and evidence under each secondary message. This information should reinforce the primary and secondary messages.

Always remember to add a call to action to your planning. This will usually be at the end of your document and will refer back to the purpose of your communication. In this call to action, you will tell your reader what you expect them to do or even what you'll do to achieve the purpose of your communication.

Your content outline will now look something like this.

What is the purpose of my communication? *To persuade the reader to buy advertising space.*
Primary message: *This advertising space will help the reader to grow their business.*
Secondary message: *Visitor traffic* **What to include:** • *Traffic to the site: daily, weekly, monthly* • *Loyal audience*
Secondary message: *Benefits of advertising on this website* **What to include:** • *Trusted website* • *Increasing brand awareness* • *Quality articles* • *Free design*

Secondary message: *Low cost* **What to include:** • *Limited-time offer* • *Advertising space* • *Cost* • *Deadline of offer*
Secondary message: *Proven results* **What to include:** • *Statistics on results achieved* • *Success stories of other advertisers* • *Projected return on investment based on these statistics*
Call to action: *I'll contact you on Monday to confirm your space. Alternatively, you can reach me anytime at (phone number) or email (include your email address, even if it's included in your email signature).*

Look at Sources

If you write without having sources or including specific research and the methodologies used to do the research, your content can appear to be only your opinion. This can make your reader more hesitant to accept your suggestions, ideas, or products. Try to include some sources in your writing, not so many that it affects the readability of your content but enough to increase its credibility. Once you've found reputable sources to use in your content, note them under all relevant messages.

Create Subheadings

Once you know what to discuss under each of your secondary messages, look at creating subheadings. They should be short, ideally not more than five words each, and tell your reader exactly what they can expect to read in that section of the content. Add your subheadings to your content outline. You will use this to arrange your content in the next step.

Arrange Your Information

When you initially identified the primary and secondary messages for your writing, you likely prioritized them. However, since then, you have given them more thought, done more research, and looked at potential sources you will use. This might make a difference in the importance of each of your messages.

Consider the importance of each of your messages again and make sure they are organized in the most logical way. By doing this now, you will create a clear plan and order before you start writing, resulting in you having to copy, paste, and delete less information once you start writing. This will also help in creating the best possible flow for your content.

Consider Your Connections

You will now have a good understanding of the messages that will be in your writing, why you need to include them, and how this can help convince your reader to accept your approach or product. Now, take some time to consider how you will make sure your document will flow.

Think of sentences you can write to connect the primary message to the secondary message, the second to the third, and so on. By doing this, you will create a natural flow in your document, and your reader will understand exactly how and why they fit together.

If you struggle with coming up with connecting sentences, it may mean that the order of your messages isn't correct. Revisit this to see if you can revise your order so that it makes more sense and flows more easily.

Your content outline will now look something like this.

<table>
<tr><td>What is the purpose of my communication?
To persuade the reader to buy advertising space.</td></tr>
<tr><td>Primary message: This advertising space will help the reader to grow their business.
Title: Start growing your business' online presence today!
Connecting sentence:
Your company is sure to benefit from the high traffic on our website.</td></tr>
<tr><td>Secondary message: Visitor traffic
Subtitle: Take advantage of our high traffic
What to include:
• Traffic to the site: daily, weekly, monthly
• Loyal audience
Sources: Traffic reporting dashboard, Customer retention report
Connecting sentence: The benefits of advertising on this website can change your company for the better.</td></tr>
<tr><td>Secondary message: Benefits of advertising on this website
Subtitle: Get these benefits
What to include:
• Trusted website
• Increasing brand awareness
• Quality articles
• Free design
Connecting sentence: I'm offering you a once-in-a-lifetime limited deal.</td></tr>
<tr><td>Secondary message: Low cost
Subtitle: Limited offer
What to include:
• Limited-time offer
• Advertising space
• Cost
• Deadline of offer
Connecting sentence:
If you're not convinced yet that this is ideal for your business, let's look at our proven results.</td></tr>
</table>

Secondary message: *Proven results*
Subtitle: *Get these results*
What to include:

- *Statistics on results achieved*
- *Success stories of other advertisers*
- *Projected return on investment based on these statistics*

Sources: *Sales data analysis, customer testimonials*
Connecting sentence: *I'm sure you'll agree with the amazing benefits your company will gain from booking this advertising space.*

Call to action: *I'll contact you on Monday to confirm your space. Alternatively, you can reach me anytime at (phone number) or email (include your email address, even if it's included in your email signature).*

Do Your Checks

You now have a good idea of how you will organize your writing and what you should include in your document. If you feel satisfied with how your thoughts have been organized, use the *Five Ws* and the *H* to double-check that you've covered the basic information your reader will need. The following questions may help you to do these checks, but don't feel limited by them. Your situation may require different questions.

- **Who?** Did you mention a specific person who will have to complete a task? Are you expecting your reader to be the "who?" Are you clear on this?

- **What?** What actions do you expect to be taken after your reader has had time to review your content? Are you clear on this?

- **When?** Are you setting strict deadlines? If not, how will your reader know when your approach will be implemented or when you'll contact them again to try and confirm the sale? If the reader agrees to the deal, when will they receive the product? If you're relaying information, when will this information come into effect?

- **Where?** Where will your approach be implemented, or where can your reader look at or receive the product should they agree to a sale?
- **Why?** This question is usually answered close to the start of your content. Why should your reader care about what you have to say? What impact will your approach or product make in their life?
- **How?** How will you implement the steps mentioned in your content? How can your reader purchase your product? How will you measure the success of the new project?

Take a Break

Once you've completed all the steps above, try to take a break from your planning. If you have enough time, leave it for a day or two; otherwise, try to focus on other tasks for at least an hour before returning to it. Don't look at your content outline while you're taking this break. Spending some time away from your outline will help you gain a new—and often objective—perspective on the information you're working with. This can help you come up with better ways of using the information you need to include in your content.

Relook and Repeat

Once your break is over, look at your outline again. Consider all the information you've included in your planning, whether it should be included in your document, and if it's currently placed in the correct order. Is there a message that doesn't seem to fit? Does it feel like something is missing? Can you think of or find better sources than the ones listed in your outline? Do all the messages connect?

If you're satisfied with your planning and your answers to these questions, you can move to the next step of starting to write. If not, you should repeat the steps above until all the information in your content outline makes sense and works well together.

Refining your outline is an important step that some of the most experienced business writers have to do repeatedly until they're satisfied with the order and flow. Don't get too stressed about how long this may take; once your outline is complete, your document is practically written. And you'll know that the content you're including is of the highest quality and value to your reader.

Tip 3 Cheat Sheet

Defining and organizing your messages before you write can help free up a lot of time later. Creating a content outline will ensure your writing flows logically and is easy for your reader to follow and understand.

- Start by doing some research. Consider the questions your reader might ask. Think about the messages you want to send to your reader.
- Once you've defined your messages, you can start to organize them. How you structure your written content will depend on the type of communication you're writing and what outcome you are trying to achieve.
- **The Pyramid Principle.** Start with the most important information first, followed by secondary messages and supporting facts and evidence.
- ***Five Ws* and the *H*.** Who, What, Where, When, Why, and How.
- **Situation–Complication–Resolution.** What's the current situation, what's changed to create the problem, and what's the proposed solution?
- **The Three-Act Structure.** Follow the general rule of thumb:
  - **Opening**
    - Start with the conclusion and what benefits your content will bring the reader.

    - Give some background as to why your suggested approach or product is ideal.

- **Main body**
    - Provide a problem statement where you discuss the challenges your reader may face and possible alternative options and why they aren't as ideal as your suggestion.
    - Next, give all the analysis you can to prove your point. Start with the technical analysis, followed by the non-technical analysis.
- **Closing**
    - Briefly summarize your reader's main challenges and how your approach or product may help them solve them.
    - If you need the reader to make a decision based on your document, be clear on what you require and by when.
    - Explain to the reader how they can direct any questions they may have to you or when you'll follow up with them.

- Based on your selected writing structure, create an outline of your primary and secondary messages, decide on subheadings, arrange your messages according to their importance, and make sure you can easily connect each message to the next one.

You should now be ready to start writing your document. The next thing you should be mindful of is the type of language you use. In Tip 4, we will explore the importance of using plain language to keep your document simple and concise.

Tip 4:
Use Plain Language

Say all you have to say in the fewest possible words,
or your reader will be sure to skip them, and in the plainest
possible words, or he will certainly misunderstand them.
–John Ruskin

In this chapter, you will learn

- why it is important to use plain language in your writing.
- how to make sure your reader will easily understand your writing.
- how to use technical language in your writing.
- how to determine the right tone of voice to use.

Have you ever received a document to read that was written in such a complicated way that you needed to use a dictionary to understand what the writer meant? Have you ever given up halfway through reading a document because it took too long? Have you ever felt dumb trying to decipher what the writer meant, wondering *Why don't I understand a word of this?* Do you want to do this to your reader?

The answer to this is most definitely a big *no*. Your goal in your business writing should be that your reader will understand what you're trying to say immediately without putting in too much effort. This will reduce the risk of being misunderstood and increase the chance of getting buy-in from your reader.

The best way to ensure you achieve this is by using plain language. Write in the same way you would talk. In short, keep your writing as simple and concise as possible without losing the message you need to convey to your reader.

Why It's Important to Use Plain Language

If you have ever wondered why using plain language is so important, you simply have to look at the statistics. According to a study by the Department of Education in the United States, about 130 million adults in this country have low literacy skills. To be exact, the reading ability of around 54% of Americans between the ages of 16 and 74 is below the level required of sixth graders (Schmidt, 2022).

Additionally, around 15% of children and adults in America have dyslexia, a learning disability that causes them to struggle to read, write, and spell (Society for Neuroscience, n.d.). Dyslexia has no correlation to a person's intelligence, and, as a result, you often find people in top positions with this condition.

Since you often won't know your reader's reading ability, do you want to overcomplicate things by writing in a way that, no matter how hard they try, they won't understand?

Plain language is a simple way to navigate your reader's potential reading challenges. This is the type of language your reader would easily be able to understand the first time they read or hear it.

Even if your reader has no reading disability, plain language will help them to read through and absorb your information faster. In the business world, where time is money, no one will want to spend an hour reading something that could've taken less than 10 minutes to understand. Also, the easier it is for your reader to understand your content, the less likely they'll have follow-up questions. If your document's purpose is to explain new methods that staff members should follow in their operations, they will also be more likely to apply these immediately if they can clearly understand your message.

You will likely also save time in writing the content, as you'll be able to write as you speak without feeling the need to add fancy words—and potentially look up the meaning of the words—to your writing. It's a win-win situation for everyone involved.

How to Write in Plain Language

Apart from using the type of words you would use when you speak, there are many other ways to ensure your language is plain and simple. Let's look at how you can achieve this.

Use Simple, Short Words

A business document isn't the type of content most people would enjoy reading in bed before going to sleep. Therefore, there is no need to be creative with puns or other literary flairs. Instead, business writing is about conveying an important message as clearly and succinctly as possible. Use familiar words as much as possible. Be concrete in your content and avoid abstract thoughts. Opt for short words that read easily instead of using long tongue twisters. In the Handy Resources chapter of this book, I'll provide you with lists of words you may want to use for maximum readability.

Explain the Actions Directly

Always explain the action taken as directly as possible in your writing. If your team is responsible for analyzing data, say it like it is, "We analyze the data." There is no need to say, "The team I work with is responsible for conducting analysis on the data provided."

Let's look at another example: If you're advertising a vacancy at your company, simply write, "Please apply for this position if you meet the requirements." *Apply* is used directly, and the reader will immediately know what to do. Don't say, "Please make an application for this position if you meet the requirements." Now, the instruction in your writing is not as explicit, and your reader might miss it.

Avoid Jargon

In many instances, jargon is used to try to impress your reader instead of informing them. Often, the overuse of jargon only results in the reader losing interest and your message being lost.

Avoiding jargon can be an effective way of using plain language when communicating with your reader. However, this doesn't mean you should lose the technical terms necessary to convey your message. This may be required when there isn't another clear and correct way of referring to something.

Let's look at an example of the difference between jargon and technical terms. If you're writing for the construction industry and you know your content will only be read by civil engineers or qualified builders, you may refer to the *phreatic surface*. However, if your content will be read by people not qualified in this field, your document will be much better understood if you simply use the term *water table*. More people will know that this is the level below the ground that is saturated with water.

Another example can be the use of *myocardial infarction*. If you use this term for people working in the medical field, they will understand what this means. However, the broader population won't necessarily know that this is simply a medical term for a heart attack. Doctors won't think less of your document if you use the term *heart attack* instead of *myocardial infarction*. And the chances of your content being understood by those without this medical knowledge will drastically increase.

Unless you're sure that your reader will understand specific terms, always opt for the easier-to-understand options. Use everyday language as often as you can. Always remember that using plain language doesn't take away from your content, whereas content filled with jargon can make it difficult to understand.

Acronyms and Abbreviations

When you want to use an abbreviation or acronym in your writing, don't assume your reader will know what it means. An abbreviation is a shorter form of a word; for example, Dr. for doctor or Jan. for January. An acronym is made up of the first letter of each word of the bigger phrase; for example, NASA for National Aeronautics and Space Administration or PIN for Personal Identification Number.

Apart from a few exceptions to this rule, always define the abbreviation or acronym the first time it's used and then add the abbreviation or acronym in brackets. After that, you can use only the abbreviation or acronym. For example, attention deficit hyperactivity disorder (ADHD) or annual general meeting (AGM).

Be careful not to use too many abbreviations or acronyms in your writing, as this can lead to confusion and misunderstandings. You can't expect your reader to take in all your well-researched content and have to keep track of 20 different abbreviations or acronyms. A general rule of thumb would be to only use abbreviations or acronyms for the three most common items in your writing. If you're using others only once or twice in your document, it will likely increase the readability if you write them out.

As with most rules, there are exceptions. If you want to use abbreviations that are commonly used and understood, you can use them without explanation. For example, there's no need to write Federal Bureau of Investigation; you can simply use FBI. Similarly, why would you use an automated teller machine if you are certain all your readers will know what an ATM is?

Place Words Carefully

You can use all the correct words, but if you put them in the wrong place in your sentence, you can create room for misunderstanding in your content. Let's look at three rules you can follow. They may seem a little confusing at first glance, but as you use them, they will become easier to apply in your writing.

- Structure your sentence using the subject–verb–object rule. The *subject* will be the *person or thing* doing the action, the *verb* is the *action word* that determines what is done, and the *object* will be the *thing that gets done*. According to this rule, you should use these three parts of the sentence as close to each other as possible; for example, "The team (subject) analyzed (verb) the data (object)." This reads much easier than when you write, "The team took on the task of analyzing the data."

Instead of this	**Write this**
The meeting about the project was held by the managers.	The managers met about the project.

- Use words such as "only" or "always" as close as possible to the word they apply to or change; for example, "You should order only the following:" instead of "You only should order the following:" The word "only" applies to what should be ordered.

Instead of this	Write this
Complete the following sections always.	Always complete the following sections.

- Put the part of your sentence that changes or limits the main part of the sentence after this main part; for example, "Complete Section A if your business qualifies for this deal." In this case, "complete Section A" is the main part or instruction of the sentence, while "if your business qualifies for this deal" will be the part that changes the main part. This reads easier than when you write, "If your business qualifies for this deal, complete Section A." If you put the limiting part of the sentence before the main part, the reader might miss the instruction altogether.

Instead of this	Write this
If you want to make use of this deal, order the product now.	Order the product now if you want to make use of this deal.

Write Short Paragraphs

Long paragraphs may demotivate your reader from continuing to read. Try to limit your paragraphs to only three to six sentences per paragraph.

Avoid discussing more than one topic in a paragraph. This can confuse the reader and result in them not understanding your content.

Make your writing interesting by varying the lengths of your paragraphs. If your content requires one paragraph to be longer, make sure your following few paragraphs are shorter. Do the same with your sentences. This will make your content seem more inviting and easier to read.

You can also improve the readability of your content by using subheadings to break it up into smaller digestible sections, bullet points, or numbered lists. We will discuss formatting your document in more detail in Tip 7.

Tone of Voice

Tone of voice is an important aspect of effective business writing. It refers to how you relay your message to your reader and how your sentences are constructed; for example, formally or informally. It can affect how your reader perceives and interprets your message, influencing how they respond.

Not everyone's talents lie in putting sentences together, and that's okay. As I've said, business writing isn't creative writing. However, there are simple ways to work on the tone of your writing without needing to sign up for writing classes.

Use Active Voice

Business writing often comes down to telling your reader what you'd like them to do. By using active voice instead of passive voice, you make this clear to your reader. In an active voice, the person who should do the action is the subject of the sentence; for example, *You must order this product.* In passive voice, the thing that is acted upon becomes the subject; for example, *This product must be ordered.* Do you see the difference? In the active example, the reader knows they must take action, but this is not as clear in the passive example.

Passive voice	**Active voice**
The report was compiled by the team.	The team compiled the report.
A meeting was held by the managers.	The managers met.

Use Present Tense

Another easy way you can improve the tone of your writing is by making sure you write in the present tense as often as you can. Present tense refers to something currently happening, past tense refers to something that has happened, and future tense refers to something yet to happen.

The present tense not only simplifies your message, it also makes it more direct and instructional. Let's look at some examples.

Present tense	**Past tense**	**Future tense**
The team is doing research.	The team was doing research.	The team will do research.

Let's look at some exceptions to this rule. When you refer to research that was done, you will likely have to write in the past tense. However, you can avoid confusion if you use the past tense strictly when referring to the research; for example, "Our research found the product to be effective."

There will also be times when you have to refer to the future tense. This is particularly the case when you refer to timelines for future forecasts in the project. Keep the use of future tense only for the things that must still happen; for example, "I'll provide the results from our research next Monday."

Use Contractions

Many people believe that contractions should be avoided due to the formality that often comes with business writing. The term "contraction" refers to a situation when two words are made shorter by combining them into one; for example, *do not* becomes *don't*, *you will* becomes *you'll*, and *it is* becomes *it's*.

Contractions are widely regarded as a way to improve the readability of written content. They can also help to make writing appear more conversational, as most people use contractions naturally when they speak. Contractions can help people to relate to written content more easily.

It is, however, important to never force contractions. Not every word that can be turned into a contraction should be. If you're unsure whether you should or shouldn't use a contraction, read your sentence out loud. If the contraction sounds natural, then go for it. If it sounds forced, write the words out in full.

Tip 4 Cheat Sheet

One of the most important aspects of writing is making sure your reader can absorb the information as easily and quickly as possible. The less time your reader spends trying to decipher what you wrote, the more likely your message will be accepted.

Using plain language can improve the odds of your written content being read and understood. Let's look at some questions you can ask yourself to make sure you're using plain language:

- Am I using simple, familiar words? Am I choosing the shortest words that are easy to read and understand?
- Am I using unnecessary jargon? Will the technical terms I'm using be generally understood by my reader?
- What acronyms or abbreviations am I using? Is it necessary to use all of them? What are the three acronyms or abbreviations that I use the most? Can I write the rest out, or does it read better with the acronyms or abbreviations? Am I defining any acronyms or abbreviations that are obvious?
- Am I writing in short paragraphs? Do I stick to one topic per paragraph? Do I vary the lengths of my paragraphs to make my writing more interesting?
- Am I using an active voice? Am I making sure my reader knows what action I want them to take? Read through your document and highlight every instance of passive voice. Then, try to change this to an active voice.
- Am I using the present tense as much as possible? If I'm using another tense, is it necessary, or can I change it to the present tense?

When delivering written content, it's essential that you don't offend your reader, no matter how unintentional it may be. In the next chapter, we'll discuss how you can make sure your writing is inclusive and accessible.

Tip 5:
Make Your Writing Inclusive and Accessible

When everyone's included, everyone wins. –Jesse Jackson

In this chapter, you will learn

- the importance of making your writing inclusive and accessible.
- how to use inclusive language.
- how to make your writing accessible to as many readers as possible.

When compiling your message, you want it to be received well by your reader. To ensure you achieve this in today's modern business environment, it's crucial that your writing is inclusive and accessible.

Inclusive language refers to the use of words and phrases that are non-offensive and non-exclusionary to different groups of people. It's the opposite of exclusive language, which can make some people feel marginalized, unimportant, or invisible. Do you want your reader to feel like they aren't included or offend them by choosing your words poorly?

Accessible writing is writing that can be easily understood and used by as many people as possible, including people with disabilities, non-native language speakers, or those with lower levels of education or literacy. It's writing that, if sent electronically, can be read by readers who use assistive technology, such as screen readers or text-to-speech software. Do you want to write something that a colleague can't read?

If you're not yet convinced about how important it is to make sure your writing is inclusive and accessible, let's look at two statistics released by the World Health Organization (*33 accessibility statistics, 2022*):

- Around 15% of the world's population has a disability of some sort.
- Approximately 217 million people globally had severe vision impairment in 2015. This number is expected to go up to 588 million people by 2050.

You should never assume that your reader will be able to access your document in the traditional format you're writing in.

Put yourself in your reader's position. Imagine you receive an email from a colleague that uses phrases you don't understand. Or, the team is referred to as a specific gender; for example, "the guys," but you're female or identify as a female. Or you have low vision and need to use technology to read an email, but it includes tables and images that aren't accessible, resulting in you missing the message. How would you feel? I know I wouldn't want to receive a document that excludes me or that I can't access.

As more and more businesses realize the benefits of creating products, services, and workplaces that are barrier-free and open to everyone, being able to write content that is inclusive and accessible is becoming a necessary skill for today's business writer.

How to Use Inclusive Language

When you use inclusive language in your writing, you're deliberately using words and expressions that won't discriminate against your readers in various ways, such as race, gender, ability, medical condition, gender and gender preferences, socioeconomic status, and culture. You're also always conscious of presenting your content in a way that your reader feels included.

If you successfully achieve this, your message will be more widely accepted, more people will understand it, and more readers will feel included in your writing. This may sound hard to do, as there are many things to be careful of. However, the more you practice using inclusive language, the easier and more natural it will become. Until that happens, here are some tips that can help guide you.

Avoid Jargon, Acronyms, and Colloquial Expressions

We've already looked at how jargon can result in a reader not understanding your writing, but this jargon can make a reader feel excluded from the message if they don't understand it. They may feel like the message wasn't intended for them or, as we've already mentioned, too dumb to understand it. You should always make your reader feel positive about what you're writing about, so creating these types of feelings in them won't help anyone.

The same goes for acronyms. Many businesses use acronyms fairly freely, as most staff members understand what they mean. However, there might be new staff members who feel excluded from this. Avoid this by explaining all acronyms.

Colloquial expressions might seem harmless; for example, referring to something as a *ballpark figure* or saying that someone has *hit the nail on the head*. However, if your reader doesn't have the same background as you or is unfamiliar with these expressions, it can cause them to feel confused or even offended. You should be especially mindful of this if you work in a global office and communicate with people from around the world.

Let's look at more expressions you should consider replacing in your writing (Forsey, 2022).

Terms to avoid	Safer terms to use
just a ballpark figure	just an estimate
knock it out of the park	did a good job
you've hit the nail on the head	you're right
in the loop	aware or informed
it should be a piece of cake	it should be straightforward, easy, or simple
in light of	because of

Be Mindful of Race, Ethnicity, Nationality, and Culture

One of the big issues with inclusivity is often centered around race, ethnicity, nationality, and culture. What something means in one culture might have the opposite meaning in another. You may think you're safe using certain terms if your reader is of the same race or nationality, but always keep in mind that you may have a secondary reader who doesn't share these similarities.

This can be a tricky one to work around, as you may not be aware of the cultural implications some phrases can have. Let's take *powwow* as an example. This term is often used to refer to a meeting or get-together. However, in some Native American cultures, this term also refers to a medicinal healer or a ritual for dancing, traditionally celebrating defeat in war (Merriam-Webster, n.d.). Do you want to risk offending a potential reader when you could simply have used the word "meeting?" Again, keep your language as simple as possible to avoid these instances.

Let's look at more terms or words often used innocently that may have specific cultural meanings and can cause offense (Forsey, 2022).

Terms to avoid	Safer terms to use
blacklist or whitelist	allow list or deny list
guru	expert, authority, or guide
minorities	marginalized groups
peanut gallery	outside opinions
tribal knowledge	institutional knowledge or background knowledge

Consider Genders and Gender Preferences

Gender pronouns are words that refer to a person's gender identity, such as "he," "she," and "they." Using the correct pronouns when referring to someone is important, as using the wrong pronouns can be hurtful and disrespectful. If you're unsure what pronouns someone uses, it's best to ask or to use gender-neutral pronouns such as "they" or "them" instead.

Being considerate of gender preferences extends to more than just using *they* and *them*. To some, the term "businessman" can be offensive. For example, even if you think your reader is a male, they may identify as female, so they may take offense when you refer to "businessman."

While on gender stereotyping, be careful not to come to your own conclusions. For example, you may write for an engineering field traditionally dominated by males or the nursing industry, historically considered a female occupation. However, it's important to avoid making assumptions about people's genders based on their professions. Always err on the side of caution and keep your writing neutral.

Here are some examples of words you should avoid, as well as replacement words that may be more inclusive (Forsey, 2022).

Terms to avoid	Safer terms to use
man or woman	person or individual
his or her document	their document

salesman or saleswoman	salesperson or sales representative
he, him, his, she, her, or hers	they, them, or theirs
man-up	be brave
female or male scientist (or any other occupation)	scientist (or any other occupation)

Be Mindful of Abilities and Medical Conditions

Another thing to consider when writing is any potential medical conditions your reader might have. Let's use autism as an example. Many people with autism are highly successful in their careers. Labeling them as *autistic* or *autistic people* will most likely offend them, as they may feel that their autism doesn't define who they are. However, talking about *people with autism* has the same meaning but a much softer impact.

The same goes for common phrases such as "turning a blind eye" or "blind spot." Your reader (or someone they know) may have low vision. Using blind in such a way can offend them, as they're well aware of the challenges a person who is visually impaired may have in their daily lives.

Always be mindful of any terms or words you use that might refer to a medical condition or a disability. To help you with this, here is a list of commonly used phrases you may want to avoid and safer terms you can use (Forsey, 2022).

Terms to avoid	**Safer terms to use**
blind spot	missed opportunity
crazy	ridiculous, unbelievable, unheard of, outrageous, or unusual
disabled or handicapped	person with disabilities
lame	uncool or cheesy
walkthrough	review or guide through
hearing-impaired	person who is hard of hearing

Use Person-First Language

This ties in with the point above about making sure your writing is sensitive to those with medical conditions. Using person-first language is generally preferred when describing a person with a disability. This means that you would use language that emphasizes the person first, before their disability or condition. For example, instead of referring to someone as being "bipolar," you can instead say "a person with bipolar disorder."

When you refer to this person as having their condition, you're using identity-first language, which then implies that their condition defines their identity. Let's look at examples of using identity-first language instead of person-first language (Cruthers, n.d.).

Identity-first	**Person-first**
disabled people	person with disability
autistic people	person with autism
blind people	person with low vision
epileptic people	person with epilepsy

It's important to note that not all individuals with disabilities prefer person-first language, and some may prefer to identify themselves with their disability first. If you can, it's always a good idea to ask your reader how they would like to be referred to and respect their preferences.

Another way you can check that you are using appropriate language when referring to people with disabilities is to check with organizations that represent those groups, as they often have guidelines and recommendations for language usage available online.

How to Make Your Document Accessible

In addition to making your content inclusive, you should ensure your document is accessible to your reader. This enables your reader to access your document regardless of any medical conditions or disabilities they may have or the program they use to read it. If your document is going to be distributed electronically, there are a few things you should be mindful of to ensure it is as accessible to your reader as possible.

If your reader has low vision or prefers to have documents read to them, they may use a screen reader or one of the various PDF readers available to read your document. These programs apply text-to-speech software that reads the document out loud. Let's look at how you make your documents accessible when your reader uses this technology.

Check Accessibility While You Work

Most programs have a built-in accessibility checker that reviews your content as you write and lets you know immediately if it determines that it might cause problems. It also gives a short explanation as to why your content might be problematic for specific readers, helping you to fix the issue and teaching you how to avoid these errors in the future.

On many programs, such as Microsoft Word, this checker usually runs automatically in the background, but you should make sure it's switched on. Depending on the program you use, you can usually find this under *Tools* or *Review* on the toolbar.

Use Built-In Title Formatting

The different screen reading programs use titles, subtitles, and headings to track reading. As much as you may want to add fancy fonts to your headings, it can result in the screen reader being unable to navigate the document properly. The easiest way to make sure your headings are accessible to the various reading programs is to use the built-in heading styles in the program you use. Also, use them in a logical order, such as Heading 1, Heading 2, and then Heading 3. Using them out of order, for example, Heading 3 followed by Heading 1, will confuse your reader.

Figure 2: Built-in heading styles in Microsoft Word.

If you need to change the fonts of the built-in headings—perhaps your company dictates you use a specific font—then modify the built-in title styles rather than create new ones. In Microsoft Word, you can do this by right-clicking on the built-in style in the toolbar and selecting *Modify* from the dropdown menu.

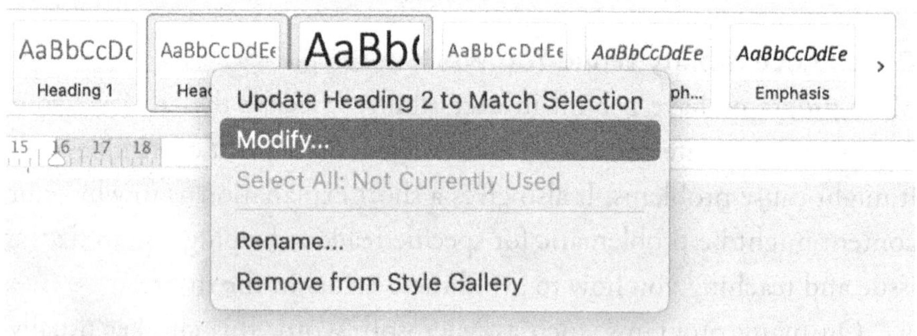

Figure 3: You can modify built-in heading styles in Microsoft Word.

Add Alt Text to Images

Images, including charts, graphs, and photos, can be an excellent way to communicate information and make your document visually appealing. However, if your reader uses screen reading technology to read your document, they may miss the meaning of your images if you haven't added alternative text, or "alt text" as it's often referred to, to your images. This text is usually read out by screen reader technology so that even though the reader can't see the images, they can still understand what they are and why you've inserted them into your document.

When adding alt text to your images, it's important to determine what type of images you're using. There are two types of images you can add to your business writing:

- **Informative images.** The purpose of these types of images is to convey a message, so it's important they include alt text. Your alt text should clearly explain the meaning of your image and any information it contains that is relevant for your reader. For example, if you include a chart in your document to show the average age of your business' customers, it's not sufficient to provide alt text that says *Chart showing the average age of Company XYZ's customers.* This doesn't tell the reader anything about the age of your customers. Instead, a more useful alt-text description would be *Chart showing 25% of Company XYZ's customers are under 30 and 75% of customers are 30 or older.* Do you see the difference? To further support the image, it's recommended that you also explain the details of any charts or graphs within the body of your text. This is helpful to both readers who use assistive technology and those who may be able to see the image but find it difficult to interpret.
- **Decorative images.** If you include an image with the sole purpose of making your page look pretty, this is called a decorative image. Decorative images don't require alt text.

How you add alt text to your image may differ depending on the program you use; a quick online search will give you the instructions to follow. In more recent versions of Microsoft Word, Excel, PowerPoint, and Outlook, you can add alt text by right-clicking on your image, selecting *Edit alt text*, and then typing your alt text description in the alt text pane.

Try to keep your alt text succinct and ensure that it clearly explains why you have included the image in your document.

Visit **support.microsoft.com** for further information about how to add alt text to images within Word, Excel, PowerPoint, and Outlook.

Make Your Tables Accessible

Tables can help present detailed information and statistics in an easy-to-read and user-friendly way, but they can be problematic when the reader uses a program such as a screen reader or magnifier, which increases the page size. Here are some ways to make your tables as accessible as possible:

- **Keep your tables simple.** Screen readers read left to right, top to bottom. Keeping your tables simple will make it easier for your reader to navigate each cell of your table.

First name	Last name	Job Title
Michael	Rowe	Managing Director
Lianne	Kim	Senior Partner
David	Singh	Head of Marketing

Figure 4: A simple table.

If, on the other hand, you create complex tables with more than two headings or you nest tables within tables, screen readers will encounter issues. For example, they may get stuck at a certain cell, and your reader will be unable to access the rest of the information within your table.

<table>
<tr><th rowspan="3"></th><th colspan="3">Team offsite</th></tr>
<tr><th colspan="2">Schedule</th><th rowspan="2">Agenda Item</th></tr>
<tr><th>Start</th><th>End</th></tr>
<tr><td rowspan="3">Day 1</td><td>9.00 a.m.</td><td>12.00 p.m.</td><td>Strategy session</td></tr>
<tr><td>12.00 p.m.</td><td>1.00 p.m.</td><td>Lunch</td></tr>
<tr><td>1.00 p.m.</td><td>4.00 p.m.</td><td>Yearly planning session</td></tr>
</table>

Figure 5: A complex table.

- **Create headers for all the columns in your table.** As a screen reader navigates left to right along a row, the content of the column headings will be read aloud. This helps your reader identify the table content and track their reading progress. As such, do not leave column header cells empty. If using Microsoft Word, you can designate a header row. This will make it easier for a screen reader to recognize that this content is in the header row. To do this, select the content in your header row, then right-click and select *Table Properties*. Select the *Row* tab, and then tick the box *Repeat as header row at the top of each page*. Be sure the *Allow row to be broken across pages* box is unchecked, as shown in Figure 6.

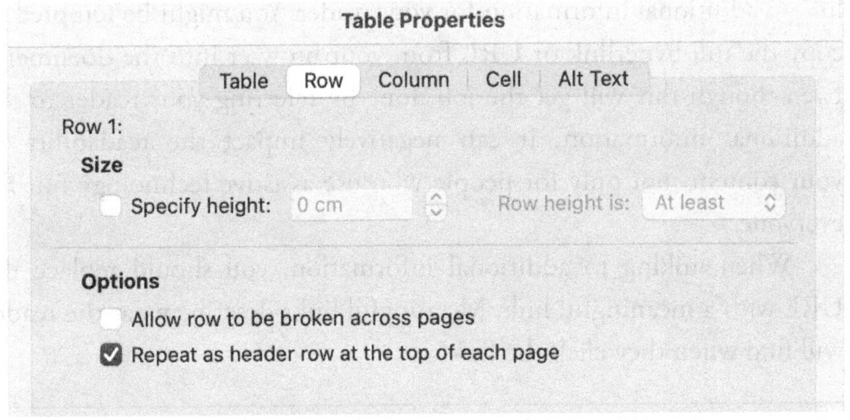

Figure 6: Table properties dialogue box in Microsoft Word showing how to define a header row.

- **Don't merge or split cells.** Most screen readers keep track of the reader's progress by counting the cells in a table. If you merge or split cells, the reader may lose track of the progress.

- **Use tables without fixed widths.** This will make it easier for readers who use programs like Microsoft Magnifier to increase the document's font size.

- **Add alt text to your tables.** Some readers may prefer to read a table description rather than every cell in the table. Adding an alt-text description lets your reader choose what works for them.

A simple way to check the accessibility of your table is to place your cursor in the first cell and, using the tab key, tab across to the next cell in the row, then the next, and so on. If you can tab your way through the entire table without getting stuck, your table should be able to be read by a screen reader.

Make Your Link Text Meaningful

If you need to keep your document as short as possible, you may want to link to additional information for your reader. You might be tempted to copy the full hyperlink or URL from your browser into the document. Even though this will get the job done by referring your reader to the additional information, it can negatively impact the readability of your content, not only for people who use assistive technology but for everyone.

When linking to additional information, you should replace the URL with a meaningful link. Meaningful links describe what the reader will find when they click the link.

Instead of using the URL	Use a meaningful link
https://www.8simpletips.com/	8 Simple Tips website
https://sharepoint/ TeamDirectory/Q4Results.com/	Team Yearly Results

It's also important to avoid using *click*-words, such as “Click here,” “Learn more,” or “See this page.” Readers with low vision using screen readers to access your document won't always have the surrounding context to help them absorb your message. The screen reader will read, “Click here, link.” As a result, the reader won't know where the link will take them. If you use a meaningful link, the screen reader will read it out, and your reader will understand what they may gain if they click on that link.

Try to create links that read as part of a sentence instead of indicating a separate link. This will help your reader stay engaged with your content and not think of using their mouse. For example, "In the report, you'll find the results of the research." You would hyperlink "results of the research." This reads better than if you write, "If you want to look at the results of the research, click here for the report." Always make sure that the link is underlined so that the reader can see that there is a link for them to click on if they wish to.

How you create a meaningful link in Microsoft Word will vary between versions. Whichever version you use, the process is simple. In more recent versions, you can follow these steps:

1. Copy the URL of the content you want to link into your document and paste it into your document.
2. Highlight this URL, right-click, and select *Link* then *Edit Link*. (In some versions, you will need to select *Edit Hyperlink*.)
3. In the *Text to Display* field, type the meaningful link text.

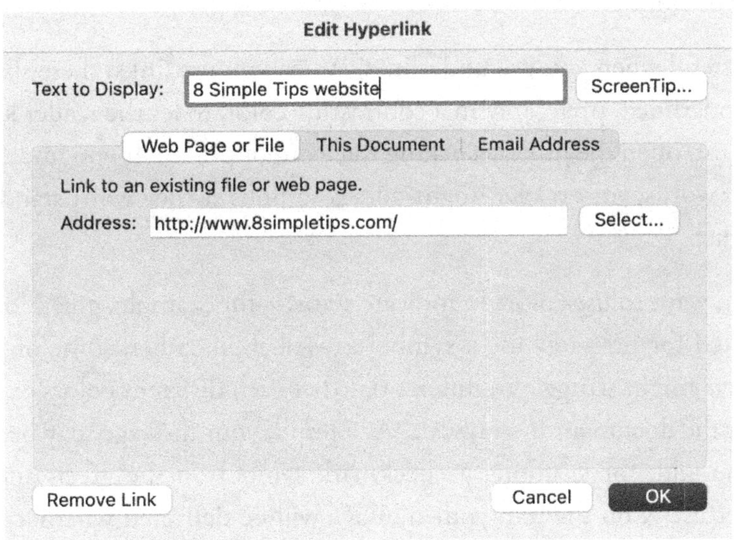

Figure 7: Edit Hyperlink dialogue box in Microsoft Word.

One final point to remember when it comes to links. If your document is being printed, it will be necessary to include the full URL address or a vanity URL—a shortened version of the URL address—so your reader can type the address into a browser to find it.

Use Accessible Fonts and Colors

You might be tempted to use pretty fonts and colors to make your document visually pleasing, but you may damage the readability of your content in the process. This can be especially disruptive for readers with low vision or reading disabilities.

Let's look at things you should consider when it comes to fonts:

- Always opt for fonts that are easy to read. Popular choices include Arial, Calibri, Georgia, and Times New Roman.
- Never type in all caps (only using capital letters), as this can create the impression that you're screaming at your reader.
- Limit the use of excessive italics, as this can decrease the legibility of your document.
- Be careful when you use underlines. When you use links, these should be underlined, preferably in a contrasting color, to let the reader know they can open the link by clicking the word or phrase. If you underline other words, your reader might miss your links as they won't stand out as much.
- If you want to use colors to indicate status—for example, green for yes and red for no—include a symbol as well. Remember, some of your readers might struggle to differentiate between different colors or may print the document in grayscale. As a result, your message may be lost. If you add, for example, a checkmark symbol on the green and an uppercase X on the red, your message will be delivered whether your reader can see the colors or not.

Adding to this, always make sure you use high-contrast colors in your document, such as black and white. If you use an accessibility checker, it will notify you if you use colors that match each other or the background too closely.

Make Your Charts and Graphs Accessible

Charts and graphs can help make large amounts of data more easily understandable by presenting it visually. Use the following techniques to make them accessible for readers with low vision or who use assistive technology:

- **Add alt text to charts and graphs.** We've already discussed adding alt text to images. It's also important to add alt text to charts and graphs. Start your alt-text description with "a chart" or "a graph" and describe what it is displaying. Once you've written your alt text, ask yourself, "Would I know what the image was showing if I couldn't see it?" If your answer is yes, you're good to go.

- **Ensure sufficient color contrast.** If you use color to distinguish between different elements of your chart or graph, ensure you have sufficient contrast between colors to maximize legibility for readers with low vision. You can also add patterns to your charts and tables to provide another way for readers who have difficulty distinguishing colors to understand the content in your visuals.

Let's look at an example of a chart that is accessible and one that's not.

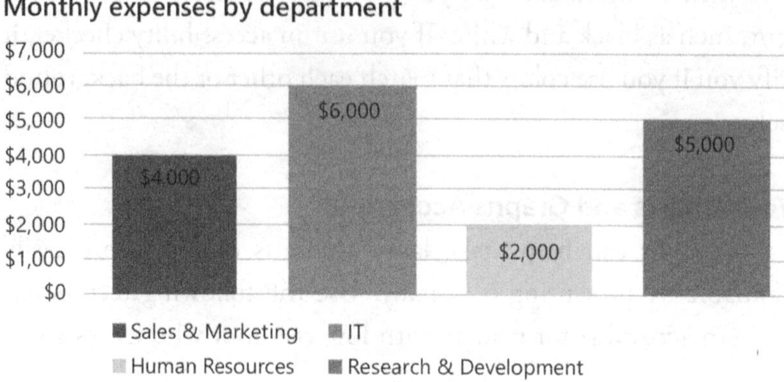

Figure 8: Example of a chart that is not accessible.

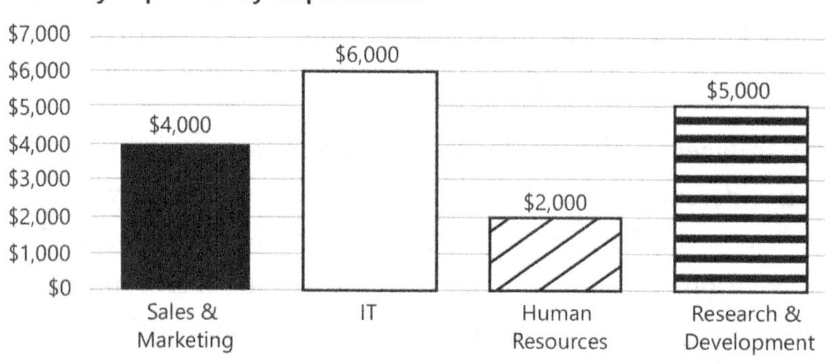

Figure 9: Example of a chart that is accessible.

In the accessible chart above, the use of high-contrast solid colors (black and white) and patterned backgrounds makes it easier to distinguish between each bar. The department names sit beneath the corresponding bar, and the expense totals sit above each bar in black text on a white background. These small but important changes make the chart easier to read and understand.

Create Enough White Space

Always make sure there is white space in your document. This can include extra spacing between your paragraphs. This will help make your paragraphs more distinct, improving your document's look and readability. It can be beneficial for readers with a reading difficulty such as dyslexia. Many people with dyslexia have reported that lines of text without enough white spaces in between merge into one another, making them close to impossible for them to read.

Avoid Using Emojis

Many people are tempted to use emojis in their content, particularly in more informal types of writing like emails. As much as using emojis can have their benefits—a simple emoji can help to bring forth the tone you want to create, such as using a smiley face to show that you intend to be friendly—they don't belong in business writing.

Emojis can also be problematic when using screen readers, as these programs often can't differentiate between emojis and punctuation marks. If you use multiple emojis in your writing, screen readers will read them all. Your innocent "How are you? ☺ ☺ ☺" will be read by a screen reader as "How are you smiling face, smiling face, smiling face." Using emojis can create the impression that you're unprofessional or even incompetent. They are best avoided.

Tip 5 Cheat Sheet

A good message can be lost if you offend readers by not using inclusive language or if your content isn't accessible. Let's recap how you can make sure you provide your reader with the best possible experience when reading your document:

- Make sure the language you use is inclusive. Ask yourself the following:
  - Am I using jargon or acronyms that my reader might not understand?
  - Do I use any colloquial expressions that might be insensitive to my reader's background?
  - Is my writing inclusive of all genders and gender preferences? Am I using gender-neutral pronouns?
  - Am I mindful of potential medical conditions or disabilities my reader might have?
- Make your document accessible to your reader no matter what program or device they use to read it. Ask yourself these questions:
  - Am I using a built-in accessibility checker? What flags is this checker raising? Am I taking the necessary action?
  - Are my tables simple? Do all my table columns have headers?
  - Am I using the built-in heading styles?
  - Do all my informative images have alt text included?
  - Are all my hyperlinks and URLs changed to links that flow with my content?
  - Am I using font types that are easily legible and contrasting colors to make my content accessible on all platforms?

Once you've made sure your content is inclusive and accessible, you can focus on the spelling, grammar, and punctuation in your writing. In Tip 6, I'll show you how to do this.

Tip 6: **Get the Basics Right**

You can have brilliant ideas, but if you can't get them across, your ideas won't get you anywhere. –Lee Iacocca

In this chapter, you will learn

- basic rules to make sure your content is free from errors related to spelling, grammar, and punctuation.

When I was young, I remember my father telling me a story about a school spelling competition he had entered. There he was, standing in front of the classroom, eagerly awaiting his word. Finally, the teacher turned to him and said, "Vacuum. I would like you to vacuum the floor. Vacuum." *Too easy*, my dad thought, as he proceeded to spell the word, "V-A-C-double U-M." A triumphant smile spread across his face. "Incorrect." said his teacher. "The correct spelling of vacuum is V-A-C-U-U-M. There is no W in vacuum."

My father learned an important lesson that day: correct spelling matters.

You may have the best possible message, know exactly who your reader is, structure your message perfectly, and use plain language, but if your writing is filled with spelling, grammar, and punctuation errors, your message won't be received well.

Making these types of errors will, in almost all instances, come across as unprofessional and create the impression that you don't take pride in your work. If you struggle with this, you're not alone.

The good news is that it's never too late to learn. However, if you do a quick online search, you may feel overwhelmed by the vast number of different rules you need to know. Therefore, I would advise you to start with one or two at a time until you understand them and can implement them easily. To help you with this, I've listed some grammatical rules with examples.

It is important to note that some grammatical rules are different among varieties of English, so it's best to follow your dialect's rules. For example, the spelling of words in British English has been absorbed from other European languages, such as French and German, whereas in American English, words are spelled mainly as you would say them. These differences aren't necessarily major—for example, the word "honor" in

American English is spelled as "honour" in British English—but getting them wrong can impact the overall quality of your content. In this book, we use American English.

Some of the rules discussed in this chapter may seem complicated and confusing, but taking the time to understand them can empower you to write faster, make fewer mistakes, and get your message across more effectively.

Spelling

Making spelling errors is one of the main reasons written work is often regarded as "rubbish," no matter how good the message may be. Later, in the Handy Resources chapter, I'll list some common spelling mistakes with tips on how you can remember the correct spelling of these words; for example, the word "stationery" (think pens, paperclips, and pencils) has an "E" for envelope. Don't confuse it with "stationary" with an "A," which means standing still. A single letter can change the whole meaning of the word.

Let's look at some other easy-to-remember spelling rules.

I, E, C, and A

One common mistake people make is when spelling words that have an IE or an EI in them. For this rule, you only have to remember these four letters to make your rhyme: I goes before E, except after C or if it sounds like an A.

- **I goes before E.** Think of words like piece, believe, field, and relieve.
- **Except after C.** If the IE follows a C, the I and the E are swapped. For example, receive, ceiling, deceit, receipt, and conceive.
- **Or it sounds like an A.** The I and the E are also swapped if combined they sound like an A. For example, neighbor, beige, and weigh.

Watch out for a few exceptions to the rule, including seize, weird, science, either, leisure, foreign, sufficient, and height.

Swap the Y for an I

If you have a word that ends in a Y, you can swap the Y for an I unless you add an *–ing*.

Original word	**Swap the Y for an I**	**Unless you add an *-ing***
cry	cried	crying
dry	dried	drying
tidy	tidied	tidying
try	tried	trying
baby	babies	babying

Making Plurals

Making words plural can often be confusing. A plural is formed when there is more than one item; for example, two reports or two teams. In most cases, you simply add an "S," while other times, you will add an "ES." The golden rule here is that only words that end in an "S," "SH," "CH," "X," or "Z" get an "ES."

- bus + es = buses
- wish + es = wishes
- blotch + es = blotches
- box + es = boxes
- spritz + es = spritzes

All the other words will only get an "S," such as cats, dogs, shoes, and skis. However, do be careful of the catchwords that don't change when they become plural. For example, fish stays fish (you don't get fishes), sheep stays sheep, and moose stays moose. If you're ever unsure, do a quick online search for the correct plural word.

U Always Follows Q

The queen always had an usher by her side. That is an easy way to remember this rule. In most instances, when you have a word starting with a Q, the letter U will follow straight after; for example, quake, equity, quote, and question. There are a few exceptions to this rule, such as qwerty, but these words are rarely used.

S Never Follows X

Many words sound as if an "S" must follow the letter "X," but this is never the case. Instead, the S-sound is replaced by a "C." Examples include excellent, excite, and excel. Be careful with exercise, which is often misspelled as excercise. Here, the X was doing so much exercise that it ran away from the C.

CK Makes a Vowel Short

Many people struggle with knowing when a word should end in a "CK" or a "K." The rule here is simple: "CK" is always used after a short vowel sound, such as sick, duck, tick, or pick. If the vowel has a long sound, you can add the "K," for example, sake, bake, sneak, and peek. There are five vowels in the alphabet: a, e, i, o, and u. The other letters are called consonants.

There are exceptions to this rule. For example, some words with a short vowel sound will end in a "K," but this is usually when another consonant is present; for example, bark, bank, and bask.

Grammar

Once you have a better understanding of how to spell words, we can look at some basic grammar rules. Grammar refers to rules and structures that determine how sentences should be constructed.

When to Use "Is," "Are," and "Am"

One of the most common mistakes people make is using words such as "is" and "are" incorrectly. Let's look at how to use these correctly:

- If you're referring to a single subject (only one), you use: is, was, and has.
- If you're referring to a plural subject (more than one), you use: are, were, and have.
- If you're referring to yourself (I), you use: am.
- The exception to this rule is that you use the word are with you, even though you generally refer to only one person.

Don't use this	Use this	Reason
The man *are* writing a report.	The man *is* writing a report.	"The man" is only one person, so it's singular.
Jack and Sandy *was* late for work.	Jack and Sandy *were* late for work.	"Jack and Sandy" are more than one, so plural.
I *is* working late.	I *am* working late.	Always use am when referring to I, never "is" or "are."
You *is* doing research.	You *are* doing research.	Even though "You" is only one person, "are" or "were" must be used.

If you can get this right consistently you will be well on your way to giving your reader content that will be accepted and understood.

Action Tense Errors

If you're using more than one verb (action word) in a sentence, you must make sure they are in the same tense. The tense you use refers to when this action takes place; for example, past tense means it has already happened, present tense means it's currently happening, and future tense means it will still happen. Let's look at some examples of common mistakes:

- **I go to the beach and swam in the sea.** Go is present tense (happens now), while swam is past tense (happened already). In most cases, you should stick to one tense. So, the sentence should be either, "I went to the beach and swam in the sea," if it happened already, or "I go to the beach and swim in the sea" (if it's happening now).

- **I eat a hamburger and drank juice.** Again, eat is present tense (happens now) and drank is past (happened already). Change the sentence to either, "I ate a hamburger and drank juice" (when you're done eating) or "I eat a hamburger and drink juice" (when you're currently eating).

Pronoun Errors

Pronouns are words such as he, him, she, her, and they. They're used to replace nouns in sentences; for example, "The man" (noun) is replaced by "he" (pronoun), and "the team" (noun) is replaced by "they" (pronoun).

- **Luke and Noah are in a team; he work well together.** "Luke and Noah" are plural (more than one), while "he" is singular (only one). "He" should, therefore, be replaced by "they." The sentences should read, "Luke and Noah are in a team; they work well together."
- **The three companies merged; all its employees were retained.** "Three companies" are plural (more than one), but "its" is singular (only one). The sentence should read, "The three companies merged; all their employees were retained."

As discussed in Tip 5, many companies prefer to be gender-neutral in their communication with staff members. As a result, many have decided to stick with gender-neutral pronouns, such as they, their, and them. To help make sure your writing is inclusive, you can also adopt this in your writing style.

Double Negatives

Be careful of using double negatives in your writing. This happens when two negative words are used close to each other to explain something. Not only does this look sloppy and unprofessional, but it also results in the opposite meaning of what you wanted to say, as two negatives cancel each other out. Let's look at examples you should try to avoid:

- **I won't do nothing.** "Won't" and "nothing" are both negatives, so what you're actually saying is, "I will do something." It would be better to say, "I will do nothing," or "I won't do something."
- **I don't want no project.** "Don't" and "no" are both negatives, so you're saying, "I want a project." Instead, you can say, "I don't want a project," or "I want no project."

Writing Numbers

When it comes to including numbers in your document, certain rules are usually applied:

- Numbers under 10 are written out; for example, one, five, or eight.
- Numbers 10 and over are used in numerical form; for example, 25, 36, and 91.
- When you use numbers under and over 10 combined in a sentence or paragraph, you can choose a uniform way to write them; for example, all in numerical form. "I will complete 20 tasks over the next 8 days so that I can have 12 days to review the document before I need to send it to 2 managers."
- When you include a number in the thousands, use a comma to separate the thousands from the hundreds; for example, 2,500 or 30,000.

The exception to this rule is when you use a number in a title. Then, using it in numerical form can improve readability; for example, "8 Simple Business Writing Tips" instead of "Eight Simple Business Writing Tips."

Punctuation

Correct punctuation will improve the readability of a sentence and can even change the meaning of your message altogether. Consider the example, "I love to eat my family and friends." If you leave the sentence like that, you're telling your reader you're a cannibal who eats their family and friends. However, if you use the correct commas, you'll change the meaning of the sentence, "I love to eat, my family, and my friends." Now, you're listing things that you love. See the difference two commas can make? Let's look at some more basic punctuation rules to help you in your writing.

Basic Punctuation

Every sentence should start with a capital letter (A instead of a, B instead of b) and end with a punctuation mark. The different punctuation marks usually used at the end of sentences are as follows:

- **Period** (.) This is used most often in standard sentences; for example, The report should be available on Friday.
- **Exclamation mark** (!) This is used only when you indicate that the sentence should be shouted when read; for example, Book now! Limited offer available now. Many people use exclamation marks to convey a message more strongly, but this is incorrect. Also, you should never use more than one exclamation mark in a sentence; for example, !!
- **Question mark** (?) This is used at the end of a question; for example, Will the managers meet this week?

Apart from starting a sentence, capital letters are also used in the names of people, places, days, or months.

Hyphen, En Dash, and Em Dash

Many people confuse the different types of dashes when they are writing. However, getting this right is easy when you understand how these little lines should be used.

- Hyphen (-) is the shortest of all the dashes. It is used to connect two or more words:
  - high-level
  - sister-in-law
  - semi-independent
  - five-year-old
  - 30-minute
- En dash (–) is slightly longer than a hyphen but shorter than an em dash. Let's look at the different times you would use this punctuation mark:
  - in the place of the word versus; for example, the Lakers–Celtics game
  - to indicate ranges in numbers and dates; for example, 12–15 people, or the 1861–1865 American Civil War
  - to show equal partnerships; for example, teacher–teacher training
  - to show the scores, votes, or directions; for example, the final score was 6–2
- Em dash (—) is the longest of dashes. It's usually used when interrupting an idea in a sentence; for example, The project—completed over the past three weeks—highlights the product's benefits.

Keep It Parallel

This simply means you should be consistent in the punctuation marks you use in your writing. This is particularly the case when you interrupt the main part of the sentence to add extra information; for example, "My team's doing research—and finding it very interesting—on the topic." The main part of the sentence is, "My team's doing research on the topic," while "and finding it very interesting" simply adds extra information.

In most forms of writing, a comma (,) or em dash (—) would be acceptable, as long as you consistently use the same punctuation mark used at the beginning and the end of the interruptions.

Instead of this	Write this
The staff members, all from the marketing department—worked together on the project.	The staff members, all from the marketing department, worked together on the project. OR The staff members—all from the marketing department—worked together on the project.

Colons and Semicolons

Many people seem to believe that colons (:) and semicolons (;) can be used interchangeably, but the reality is that they function in entirely different ways. Let's look at the two punctuation marks:

- **Colon.** This is used to introduce a list of things. For example, To complete the transaction, you'll need: your smartphone, your credit card, proof of address, and proof of identification.
- **Semicolon.** This is used when you've connected two independent clauses or when you're separating things on a list that already includes commas. For example:
    - I have included the statistics; however, you don't need them.
    - The project will run in Los Angeles, CA; Denver, CO; and Austin TX.

The Use of Commas

Commas can be a tricky punctuation mark to get right. As long as you get the basics right and your use of commas helps to ensure your message is understood, you should be okay.

The basic rule of thumb when it comes to commas is to use them when you're listing items or separating phrases in a sentence. For example:

- I need to buy pens, scissors, a stapler, and a calculator.
- If you order this product, we will deliver it next week.

Parentheses Add Information

Parenthesis (often referred to as "brackets") and em dashes are often used in similar ways, as they help to include words that aren't part of the original clause of the sentence. One way to know when to use which is to consider if the extra information results in an interjection or a pause. If this is the case, you may opt to use an em dash. If the extra information simply adds information to your point, parentheses can be used. For example:

- If you order this product (and you know you really want to), we will deliver it next week.
- The report's appendices will include all the statistics (which you'll find very interesting) of the research that was done.

Apostrophes

A common mistake many people make when it comes to apostrophes is to use them to indicate plurals (more than one); for example, shoe's or light's. This is incorrect. Apostrophes actually only have two uses: to indicate missing letters or to show possession. Let's look at some examples:

- Words like don't, haven't, or it's.
- Don't take Jack's ideas (The ideas belong to Jack).
- It's Susan's project (The project belongs to Susan).

Tip 6 Cheat Sheet

Delivering written content filled with even the most basic grammatical errors may create the impression that you're unprofessional and don't take pride in your work. If you follow the basic rules to avoid the most common mistakes people make, you will be well on your way to creating written content that your reader will appreciate. Let's recap three important rules for spelling, grammar, and punctuation:

- **Spelling**
  - I goes before E (believe), except after C (receive) or when it sounds like an A (neighbor).
  - If you have a word that ends in a Y, you can swap the Y for an I unless you add an "ing."
  - If you are making a word plural, only words that end in an "S," "SH," "CH," "X," or "Z" get an "ES."
- **Grammar**
  - Is, was, and has are for singular; are, were, and have are for plural, and am is for I.
  - Every sentence must start with a capital letter (T instead of t), followed by a noun (man) and a verb (writes), and end in punctuation; for example, "The man writes."
  - Write your numbers up to nine in full, and use numerals for 10 and above.

- **Punctuation**
    - Know when to use hyphens (-), en dashes (–), and em dashes (—).
    - Use commas to list things and to separate different phrases in a sentence.
    - Apostrophes are only used to indicate a missing letter or to show possession.

When you're delivering written content, it's important to make sure you format your document in a way that will improve its readability. In Tip 7, we'll explore some best practices for formatting your content.

Tip 7:

Format Your Content for Maximum Readability

This report, by its very length, defends itself against the risk of being read. –Winston Churchill

In this chapter, you will learn

- best practice for paragraphs, fonts, and spacing.
- how to use lists effectively in your document.
- how to use visuals to enhance your communication.
- key elements that should be included in your communications.

In general, business executives don't have time to read lengthy documents, especially when they can glance through a document and pick out only the sections that apply to their roles in the business. If you fail to attract their attention and break the content into manageable chunks, you'll likely lose their interest, and your message won't be absorbed.

Since there are various types of business documents, it's important to write the document in a format that improves readability. Other things to consider are your font (as I've already mentioned), spacing, and when to use numbered or bulleted lists. Doing these things right will get you closer to ensuring that your document will be read, understood, and accepted.

Most word processing software or programs will have formatting tools to create professional documents. The two most popular choices are Microsoft Word and Google Docs for documents and Microsoft PowerPoint for creating presentation slides.

Many of the tips we've discussed in the previous chapters can be applied to improve the formatting of your document, such as structuring your document correctly (Tip 3) and making your document accessible to your reader (Tip 5). There are, however, more things you can look at to provide your reader with a document that's easy to read.

Paragraphs, Fonts, and Spacing

The overall look of your document can determine whether your reader makes an effort to understand your message or whether it will be discarded after only a quick glance. Always make sure your document appears to be properly structured and easy to read.

Let's look at some basic rules you can follow to create the perfect spacing between your paragraphs. You can set your word processor or program to these settings, usually located under *Format* in the toolbar.

- Don't indent your paragraphs. This is often used in more creative writing styles or when space is limited, such as in magazines, newspapers and books.
- Use a line spacing of 1.5 within paragraphs. This provides enough space for the text to be easily readable while allowing for efficient use of space on the page.
- Maintain a line spacing of 2 between paragraphs to distinguish between paragraphs.
- Either justify or left-align your text. Left alignment is usually preferred as it avoids large gaps between letters. Justified formatting can be more appropriate for certain types of content like books and newspapers.

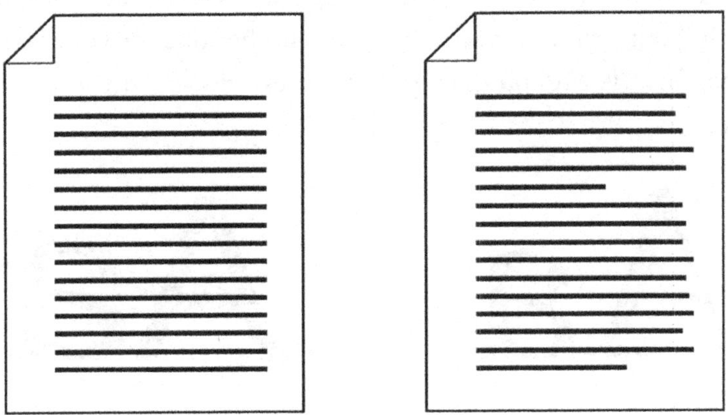

Figure 10: Justified text (shown left) and left-aligned text (shown right)

- Keep your body copy font size at either 10 or 12 points, depending on your font type. Headings and subheadings should be bigger. You can use the following suggestions as a guide:
    - Title: 25 point and bold
    - Subtitle: 23 point and italics
    - Heading 1: 18 point and bold
    - Heading 2: 16 point and bold
    - Heading 3: 14 point and italics
- Use fonts that are easy to read. Arial and Times New Roman are the most popular choices, as they are universal fonts across different types of computers. A general recommendation for choosing your font is as follows:
    - If you're writing for print, use a serif font like Times New Roman. This type of font has short strokes at the edges of the letters.
    - If you're writing for online purposes or doing presentations, you use a sans-serif font, such as Arial. This type of font doesn't have these short strokes at the edges of its letters.
- Always limit the number of fonts you use. You should stick to one font in your text and, if you have to, another one for your headings. Remember, you're producing a business document, not a party invitation.

Figure 11: The serif font on the left has strokes at the edges of the letters. The sans-serif font on the right doesn't.

Using Lists

Using lists can improve the readability of your document. It can help convey your information and break down paragraphs, allowing for more white space in your document. First, however, it's important to know what type of list to use. There are, generally, two types of lists: bulleted and numbered.

- **Bulleted lists.** Use this type of list when all the items on your list are of equal importance. For example:
  - To create a work-life balance in your life, you should do the following:
    - eat a healthy diet
    - drink plenty of water
    - do regular exercise
    - get eight hours of sleep every night
- **Numbered lists.** This is the type of list you use when the order or sequence of your lists matters or when you list steps to take. For example:
  1. Open your document.
  2. Type your message.
  3. Ensure your formatting is correct.
  4. Save your document.
  5. Send the document to your reader.

Use Visuals to Enhance Your Message

Having visuals or imagery can help enhance the point you're making in your writing. Also, your visuals can help break text, making it more interesting for your reader. As discussed earlier, always remember to add alt text to your informative images and use visuals to support your message without relying solely on them to provide the message. Types of visuals you might consider using include the following:

- charts
- diagrams
- graphs
- maps
- tables
- photographs
- drawings

Key Elements of Business Documents

Regardless of the type of communication you are compiling, specific things should be included in your document. In the Best Practice Examples chapter, we will look at some particular aspects to keep in mind when writing different types of content, including emails, letters, and meeting agendas. Let's look at things you should ensure are always in your communication:

- **Date of communication.** In a formal letter, you should write the date at the top of your document. Emails are automatically dated, so it's not necessary to include the date in your message.
- **Contact information of your reader.** The reader's name, address, and contact details should be included in a formal letter. If you're writing an email, the reader's email address will automatically be included, so it's not necessary to repeat this.
- **Your contact information.** This should be included in your communication regardless of the type of communication you're doing. If you're writing a letter, have this at the top. In an email, your contact information should be included either underneath your name when you end the communication or in your email signature if you have one.
- **Your position in the company or job title.** It's essential to let the reader know who you are. Email signatures usually include this information; otherwise, you can include it at the bottom under your name.
- **Details on the company you work for.** This will include the physical address of either your office or your company's head office, the contact number for the head office, the company registration number, and, if needed, the names of the board of directors. If you're using the company's letterhead, this information will likely already be included.

- **Opening salutation.** You should always greet your reader. How you do this will depend on the type of document you're writing and its formality.
  - If you don't know who your reader is, you can start with: To whom it may concern
  - If you're writing a formal letter, you can include the reader's title and surname. For example, Dear Mr./Mrs./Ms./Dr. Smith. Or if you want to be formal and gender neutral and the person you're writing to doesn't have an academic title, you can use their name and surname; for example, Dear John Smith.
  - If your letter is informal, you can omit the title and surname. For example, Dear John.
- **Your message.** Use one of the writing structures detailed in Tip 3 as a guide.
- **Closing salutations.** This comes just before your name and signature at the bottom of your document. Depending on the formality of your document, this can include one of the following:
  - Respectfully yours
  - Yours sincerely
  - Cordially
  - Respectfully
  - All the best
  - Regards
- **Your signature.** If you're writing an email, your email signature will be sufficient. If you're writing a letter, you may want to consider adding either an electronic version of your signature, or printing the document, signing it, and scanning it before sending it to your reader.

Tip 7 Cheat Sheet

Formatting your document properly will help to ensure that your reader receives a document that is easy to read. Let's look at questions you can ask yourself to make sure your formatting is maximized for readability:

- Are my paragraphs aligned and spaced correctly?
- What font and font size am I using? Is it easy to read?
- Am I using numbered lists only when the order or sequence of the points is important? Am I using bulleted lists for the rest?
- Could imagery and visuals make my document more engaging?
- Am I including everything that should appear on a business document?

Once you've made sure that your document is written in plain language, your message is clear and accessible to your reader, and your document is formatted correctly, you can move on to the final tip: Edit your work.

Tip 8:
Edit Your Work

The ear, not the eye, is the final editor. –Donald M. Murray

In this chapter, you will learn

- why you should do three editing passes on your writing.
- what basic steps you should follow in editing your work.
- why and how you should ask someone to be your editing buddy.
- what editing tools you can use.

You've completed your writing. You know what you want to say, you've structured your messages, used plain and inclusive language, and formatted your writing so that your document is accessible and easy to read. You're now one step away from sending your content to your reader. This final step is almost as important as writing your content: editing.

No matter how good a writer you may think you are, you'll likely make mistakes you either aren't aware of or didn't pick up while writing. Also, it often happens that you're so involved in your writing that you don't realize you're leaving important information out. You know what your message is supposed to say and have all the background knowledge, so you may not notice mistakes or omissions.

While it can be ideal to hire a professional proofreader, this may not always be possible. Teaching yourself how to edit your work and what tools you might find helpful can go a long way in checking your work. Ultimately, don't forget what potentially may be your most important tool: your ears. As Pulitzer Prize-winning journalist Donald M. Murray explains, listening to your content can help you to pick up on mistakes and problematic sentence constructions.

Three Pass Edits

Most professional editors recommend doing three passes on a document to correct mistakes and ensure all your writing is clear, concise, and error-free. Let's look at things you should check for in these three passes.

The First Pass

This is often referred to as the big-picture edit. In this pass, you'll look at your document overall to make sure your headings are strong and describe the following paragraphs effectively. You should pay attention to your introduction to make sure it's effective in grabbing your reader's attention. Then, you'll look at your content's flow to ensure it's logical and easy to follow. Next, look at your conclusion. Does it summarize your main points and bring your reader to the steps they need to follow? Does it include a call to action?

Lastly, you'll look at the overall formatting of your document. Is there enough white space in your document? Does your document appear easy to read? Does it contain everything the type of writing would require?

The Second Pass

The second pass is where you'll get down to the specific details in your document. In this pass, you'll check for any grammatical errors you may have made. Take it line for line and double-check the spelling of any words you may be unsure of. Use the basic rules in Tip 6 to make sure you fix as many errors as possible. Are there any weak verbs or adjectives you can replace with stronger ones? Are you using active voice instead of passive voice? Are you using inclusive language?

Check for any uncertain language you might have used. Examples of this may include phrases such as "seems to be" or "might be a reason for." Depending on the document you're writing, these types of phrases could give the reader the impression that you're unsure of yourself or make you sound indecisive. This will weaken your message.

Look out for repetition. While you're writing, you may not realize that you're mentioning the same points more than once. Look at your paragraphs. Do they each contain one idea or topic? Are you using data, statistics, or quotations to back up your points? Have these been cited and referenced correctly?

The Third Pass

The third and final pass gives you a last check to make sure your document is ready to be sent to your reader. Go over the edits you've made in the previous two passes and check that you haven't changed your message's meaning and that it's still grammatically correct. Make sure your sentences vary in length to make your content more interesting to your reader. Are there any unnecessary spaces in your document? If you're using page breaks, are they in the correct places?

Next, review the tips discussed in Tip 5 to ensure your document is accessible to your reader. If your word processing program has an accessibility checker, run it again to make sure nothing is flagged as problematic.

Basic Steps to Follow to Edit Your Document

Doing three editing passes on your document may help you eliminate many of the potential mistakes you may have made. Let's look at four more tricks you can try to help you identify mistakes.

Read in a New Format

Reading your document in a new format or on a different device can be helpful. For example, if you're working in Google Docs, download it as a Microsoft Word file and check your work there, or convert your Word document to PDF format to check. If you have a tablet, you can send it there to look at your work. You can also print your document and look at it on paper.

Doing this will give you a different perspective—almost that of an outsider—allowing you to view your document more critically. If you've changed it to a different format, it can also help to change the font type and size on this different format to give it a different look. This can be useful for picking up on mistakes you may have missed.

Take a Break

If you have the luxury of time, take a break from your writing, even if it's just for a few hours, or let it rest overnight (the longer, the better). While you're writing, you get involved in your content, making it extremely difficult to edit your work thoroughly. Creating this distance between you and your document can help you to identify more mistakes or phrases that sound or read awkward, as you'll look at it with fresh eyes.

Read It Out Loud

Let's go back to Murray's advice. Listening to your work can be a fantastic editing tool, as you'll discover the rhythm of your writing and make sure that it flows and that your language is plain and simple. If you struggle to read and understand specific sentences, you'll know they are poorly worded and should be changed.

If you don't want to read the entire document out loud, most word processing programs have read-out-loud options, where your document will be read back to you. The computer voice in these programs can sound strange, so if this doesn't work for you, revert to reading it yourself or ask a colleague to read it for you.

Have an Editing Buddy

Apart from asking someone to read your document out loud for you, it can be extremely valuable to ask a colleague or friend to be your editing buddy. This person doesn't necessarily have to be a professional proofreader (although this would be the first prize); just having a fresh pair of eyes can help to highlight sections where your message might not be as clear as you thought it was.

You can ask your editing buddy to review the entire document in general, pay specific attention to your message in certain sections, do a grammar check if they've got a good command of grammar, spelling, and punctuation, or simply give general feedback.

Don't be overly sensitive when it comes to the feedback they give. Remember, you've asked them to review your document to improve it. Don't take what they say to heart. You also don't have to change the entire document simply because they recommend some changes. Instead, consider their suggestions and implement what you believe would improve the document.

Tools to Use

There are many different programs available to help you edit your work. While most word processing programs, such as Google Docs and Microsoft Word, have built-in spelling and grammar checks, you can also use external programs to check your work. Some of the most popular free proofreading tools are Grammarly, ProWritingAid, WhiteSmoke, and Ginger.

These tools flag common writing and grammatical errors, which can be extremely helpful in correcting some of your mistakes. Unfortunately, they are not always 100% accurate and may flag a suggestion you know isn't correct in the context of your content. Go over their suggestions and choose which ones you want to implement. Also, always remember to set them in the language or vernacular you need to use. For example, English (US) if you're using American English and English (UK) for British English.

When you're unsure of how to spell words or if you're looking for synonyms to avoid using the same word too often, Merriam-Webster is a fantastic online dictionary. It is widely recommended by many publishing companies.

Tip 8 Cheat Sheet

Editing your work is the final step you need to take in making sure your document is ready for your reader. In this phase, you'll fix any grammatical mistakes you may have made and change sentences that might read awkwardly. Let's recap how you can edit your work effectively:

- Make three editing passes on your document to look at formatting and fixing mistakes.
- Read your document in a different format, as this can give you an "outsider's perspective" and help you to find more errors.
- Take a break from your document and look at it again later with fresh eyes.
- Read your document out loud and be mindful of any sentences you struggle to read.
- Ask a friend to be your editing buddy. Remember, you don't have to implement all the changes they recommend. Only change what you agree with.
- Use a proofreading tool, such as Grammarly, to check your work.

You've now completed all the steps to improve your business writing and understand the importance of and how to implement the eight simple tips to improve your content. Next, we will take a look at different types of business writing, when to use them, and what should be included in each.

Best Practice Examples

The most valuable of all talents is that of never using two words when one will do. –Thomas Jefferson

In this chapter, you will learn

- the different types of business letters.
- four common business documents and what each should include.
- tips on writing effective emails.
- how to make powerful PowerPoint slides.
- how to write a post on social media.

In your work, you may be expected to write many different types of communication, all with their own rules and things that should be included in them. While the tips provided already will be extremely helpful in making sure you structure and write your content correctly, there may be times when you may have to adjust your writing to suit the type of document you're writing.

Keeping track of the requirements of all the different types of business letters, emails, meeting agendas, and posts on social media can take time and effort. To help you with this, I've included a list of the types of communications used most often, their purposes, and what should be included in each type.

Types of Business Letters

Writing a business letter isn't always as simple as remembering to include dates and addresses. Various types of letters are used daily. They can be sent as physical letters or via email. It's important to identify the kind of letter you're writing so that you know what should be included in your content. Once you've done this, refer back to what you should include in all types of business letters provided in Tip 7.

- **Cover letters.** This letter accompanies something else, such as a parcel or a report. The purpose is to describe the item or report that is enclosed, the reason why this is sent to your reader, and what you'd like your reader to do with it.

- **Thank-you letters.** This type of letter aims to build a relationship with your reader. Start your letter by stating clearly that the purpose is to thank them; for example, for ordering your product or accepting your proposal. State what impact this will have and, if they've ordered something, when they'll receive it. Close with a second expression of gratitude.

- **Complaint letters.** This letter will show your reader that you're not pleased with an item or something they've done. Be careful not to come across as angry or aggressive. Explain the reasons for your unhappiness and suggest steps that can be taken to correct the situation.

- **Complaint acknowledgment letters.** This letter is sent to acknowledge that a complaint has been received. Always be humble in this type of letter and use this as an opportunity to build relationships, not to burn bridges. Tell the reader that their complaint will be investigated and when they can expect to be contacted or when the situation should be rectified. Include contact details should the reader have questions or concerns.

- **Complaint outcome letters.** This letter is sent to a reader when an investigation into their complaint has been completed. Include a description of the reader's complaint to show you understand their issues. Detail what you have discovered in your investigation as succinctly as possible. If the outcome is in the reader's favor, describe how you will address their issues or what you can offer them, for example, a refund or replacement. Include contact details for the reader to follow up should they have any questions about the outcome.
- **Bad-news letters.** Use this letter to soften the blow, no matter how bad the news may be that you have to share. Start by elaborating on how the reader is valued and what impact your business relationship with them has made. Then, break the bad news in an empathetic but clear way. Provide information on how you may further assist the customer.
- **Acknowledgment letters.** After you've received an item or report from someone, acknowledge this by sending them a letter to thank them. This type of letter can also be sent if a report or item you've sent to your reader contains an error. You can then use this type of letter to acknowledge this and inform the reader if you're going to replace the item or issue a second report in which you'll correct your error.
- **Memorandums.** This type of communication is usually used to inform stakeholders of your company (internal and external) of important news, or noteworthy decisions that were made. Get straight to the point with this type of communication. You don't have to include salutations in this type of letter. Simply state the reason for the memorandum, the information that should be shared, and possibly the impact this might have on your reader.
- **Congratulatory letters.** As the name suggests, the purpose of this letter is to congratulate your reader on something. Tell your reader why you want to congratulate them. Keep it concise and avoid sounding over-the-top in how you congratulate them, as this might create the impression that you're mocking your reader.

- **Sales letters.** The purpose of this type of letter is to convince your reader to take a specific action, such as ordering your product. Start your letter with an enticing hook to grab your reader or a specific call to action. Give them the benefits of agreeing to the sale and how long it will take them to receive the product. Make sure your details are clear in the letter so they will immediately know how to communicate with you or how they can order your product.

- **Order letters.** These letters are often referred to as purchase orders. They are used to order or buy an item or service. This is a legal, transactional type of document. You should always retain these types of letters as proof of purchase.

- **Inquiry letters.** If you need to request specific information or an item from someone, you will send an inquiry letter. Start by explaining why you're contacting the reader or why they're the best person to assist you. Then, state precisely what you need, why, and by when. Thank your reader in advance for their assistance.

- **Resignation letters.** As the name suggests, this letter is used to announce your resignation from your company. State that you are leaving the company and when your last day in your current position will be. Always remember to thank your reader for the impact they've had on your career.

Common Business Documents

Depending on the business or industry you work in, you may be required to write different types of documents. To help you do this, I have included four of the most common business documents and what you should include in each.

Meeting Agendas

The agenda of a meeting is the document in which you plan how the session will run and inform the other participants of what will be discussed. This can help everyone prepare for the meeting. Having a proper meeting agenda can also help reduce the anxiety you or other participants may experience, resulting in calmer discussions and better decision-making.

Before you compile the agenda, you can inform all the participants that you've started with the planning and that if they want to add any points to the agenda or have any questions regarding the upcoming meeting, they can send them to you via email. Give a deadline for their input so you can compile the agenda ahead of time. Let's look at the key elements of an effective meeting agenda:

- **Title.** Start with the title 'Meeting agenda' so that all your readers will know what the document is.
- **Meeting name.** Include a descriptive name for your meeting, for example, Quarterly Planning Session.
- **Administrative details.** Include the date, time, and location of the meeting.
- **Meeting participants.** List the people who will be attending the meeting.
- **Meeting purpose.** Make the purpose of the meeting clear by listing the goals for the meeting.

- **Welcome and introductions.** Include time for introductions and list who will lead this—usually the meeting leader or host.
- **Agenda items.** List the topics for discussion. For each agenda item, include the following:
  - **Time.** Estimate how many minutes you expect to spend discussing the agenda item, or include the actual time, for example, 11.00 a.m.–11.15 a.m.
  - **Action item purpose.** Say what you'd like to achieve during this discussion on this agenda item, such as "Share information," "Track progress," or "Make a decision."
  - **Presenter.** List the person who will be presenting the agenda item during the meeting.
  - **Remarks.** List any remarks you have on the agenda item, such as "discuss the previous financial statement," "look at the projections for the coming months," or "discuss resources." Numerous remarks can be discussed during the meeting depending on the type of agenda item and how long you plan to spend on each item.
- **Summary.** Give the leader or host time to summarize the meeting. Detail any additional discussion points to be covered before the meeting is closed. Include the time you plan to devote to closing the meeting and who will be closing the meeting.
- **Attachments.** Include any documents or additional reading participants may require for the meeting.

Meeting Minutes

Meeting minutes are a written record of the discussions, decisions, and actions taken during a meeting. They serve as a historical record of the meeting for future reference and to inform future planning and, as such, are essential business documents.

When writing meeting minutes, you should include the following:

- **Title.** Start with the headline "Meeting minutes."
- **Meeting name.** Include a descriptive name for your meeting. This should match the name in your meeting agenda.
- **Administrative details.** Include the date, time, and location of the meeting.
- **Meeting participants.** List the people who attended the meeting.
- **Apologies.** List the people who were absent from the meeting.
- **Outcomes.** Detail succinctly and accurately what was discussed for each agenda item (following the order set out in the meeting agenda), what decisions were made, and what next steps were agreed upon.
- **Adjournment.** List the date and time the meeting was adjourned.
- **Approval.** Include the name and signature of the person responsible for approving the minutes and the date they were approved.

You should send meeting minutes to all participants as soon as possible after the meeting while the discussions and decisions are still fresh in everyone's minds. In general, sending out the meeting minutes within 24 to 48 hours after the meeting is recommended.

Standard Operating Procedure

A Standard Operating Procedure (SOP) is a critical business document that details how a task should be performed within an organization, ensuring consistency and efficiency. If you are tasked with writing an SOP, below is a guide to what you should include:

- **Title.** Your title should clarify to the reader what task the SOP relates to. This is not the time to use attention-grabbing headlines that leave your reader guessing. Instead, be clear and direct.
- **Date.** Include the date the SOP was created or revised.
- **Purpose.** This should be a clear and concise statement outlining the objective of the SOP and why it is necessary.
- **Scope.** Detail the area of application for the SOP and include any limitations or exclusions.
- **Responsibilities.** Specify who performs the tasks outlined in the SOP.
- **Materials.** List the equipment, materials, and resources required to perform the task.
- **Step-by-step procedure.** Here you will provide detailed instructions on the steps required to perform the task, including potential hazards and safety measures. Ensure that all steps are ordered logically and are numbered.
- **Quality control measures.** Include a description of measures in place to ensure the quality of the task output.
- **References.** List relevant documents or sources used to create the SOP.
- **Approval.** Make sure to include the name and signature of the person responsible for approving the SOP and the date it was approved.

Business Reports

Business reports aid decision-making and problem-solving by providing information, insights, and recommendations on specific business issues. You may come across several types of business reports in your business writing, including financial statements, market research reports, operational reports, progress reports, and feasibility reports.

As we discussed previously, the content of your report will vary depending on your topic, industry, and reader. However, as a guide, listed below are key elements you can include in a business report:

- **Title.** In addition to including the title of the report, you can also include a sub-title. In the sub-title, consider adding an element of intrigue to pique the reader's interest.
- **Date.** Include the date the report was published.
- **Name of the report author/s.** Include the names and titles of all authors.
- **Executive summary.** Provide a brief overview of the purpose and main findings of the report, including key recommendations and conclusions.
- **Introduction.** Give a brief explanation of the context and background of the report, including the scope and objectives of the report.
- **Methodology.** Describe the research methods used to gather data and information for the report.
- **Findings.** Present the key research findings, including data, statistics, and analysis.
- **Discussion.** In this section, you provide a detailed discussion of the findings and their implications, including an examination of trends, patterns, and relationships. As discussed in Tip 2, ensure you answer your reader's questions.

- **Recommendations.** Based on the report's findings, list your recommendations for further action or improvement.
- **Conclusion.** Summarize the report's main conclusions, including the implications for future action or decision-making.
- **Appendices.** Include additional information or supporting materials, such as graphs, charts, tables, and references, that provide further context or detail for the report in the appendices.
- **References.** List the sources used in the report, including books, articles, websites, and other sources. This will give credibility to your report.

Writing Effective Emails

When writing a business email, it's important to remember that many business executives may easily receive hundreds of emails every week. Therefore, it's essential to make sure that your email stands out from the rest. Since your reader will only see your name and subject line when they receive your email, it's important to have the best possible subject line. Doing this lets your reader know precisely what the email is about and why they should open it. A good subject line will also help your reader find your email if they need to refer to it. Some tips on how to do this include the following:

- Keep your subject line as short as possible; for example, under 40 characters or at most seven words.
- Avoid spam words such as "free" or "buy now." This can result in your email automatically ending up in the reader's spam folder.
- An open-ended question can lure the reader into opening your email; for example, "What is the one product you can't live without?"

- Include a deadline in your subject line; for example, "Now or never" or "last chance."
- Draw them in with a teaser instead of a punchline.
- Some readers respond best to an explicit instruction or call to action in the subject line; for example, feedback is required by Friday.
- Make an announcement in the subject line.

In addition to using a good subject line, there are other ways to increase the chances of your reader opening and reading your email:

- Keep the email short. Many readers won't have hours to spend reading their emails. If you keep your writing as succinct as possible, your reader will feel more motivated to read it.
- Greet your reader in an appropriate way. Start your email by appropriately greeting your reader; for example, Dear Dr. Smith, Dear John Smith, or Dear John. End your email with a call to action, salutations, and email signature, which should include your job title, contact details, and company details.
- Include receivers' details. If you send your email to more than one recipient, you might want to inform all your readers who the other recipients are by adding, "This email is being sent to all the sales representatives in the sales department." Even though your reader will likely be able to see who the other recipients are in the "To" field, it doesn't always show, and your readers might not make an effort to look in that field.
- Use bullet points. Emails are often scanned through instead of read closely. Bullets make it easier for the reader to absorb your message.
- Stick to one topic per email. This will help you to get your message across quicker. If you need to include more than one topic, prioritize them and put your most important message at the top.

- Avoid any urges to include emojis. You might think they look cute, but the only purpose they really serve is to make you appear unprofessional.
- If you need to use attachments, make this as easy as possible for your reader. Many won't go to the trouble of opening an attachment, so copy the most important part into your email. This way, your reader will know what content is in the attachment and can decide whether they want to open it or not.

Using PowerPoint Effectively

There's nothing worse than sitting in a meeting while the presenter reads their slides word-for-word. It's not only boring, it's a waste of your reader's precious time. Avoid this trap by using your slides more effectively. Small changes can have a big impact on how your reader will receive your slides. Let's look at some tips to consider:

- Limit the text you use on your slides. Stick to using only keywords or phrases while you explain the rest during your presentation.
- Make sure your chosen theme has plenty of white space. Do this by limiting the amount of text and visuals on a slide.
- Use the preformatted slide layouts to make sure they are accessible.
- Keep animations and transitions plain. Doing a presentation is about impressing your audience with your research and knowledge rather than your creative skills.
- The optimal text size is between 24 and 32 points. The smallest you should ever go is 18 points.
- Use an accessible font and make sure your font color is in contrast with your background color.
- Use the built-in bullet function. Don't try to create bullet lists using hyphens.

- Never use URLs in your presentations. Edit them to create meaningful links the reader can easily understand.
- Using visuals in your presentation can help you to bring your message across more clearly, as one picture can replace what you might need hundreds of words to describe. Choose your images carefully and avoid clip art as it can look cheap and unprofessional. Alternatively, you can search for free, royalty-free images online. Always remember to add alt text to informative images.
- As discussed in Tip 5, use simple table structures and avoid merging or splitting cells.
- Try to keep your presentation as succinct as possible. If you are presenting your slides in person or online, remember that your slides are there to support what you say, not do the talking for you.

Posting on Social Media Platforms

If you're responsible for updating your company's social media platforms, you should relay positive messages and be professional in every post you make. To increase traffic on your platforms and boost your company's online profile, it is important that you create frequent posts, as this will boost the platform's algorithm in your favor. Without going into the mechanics of these algorithms, it's generally believed that at least one post a day should do the trick.

Now, you might wonder where you'll find the time to create meaningful content every day. This is where the 10-4-1 rule comes in. For every 15 posts you create, 10 should be copied from industry experts (and referenced properly), four should be created by yourself, and one should be a call to action.

- **Ten posts from experts:** This will help you to stay relevant, and if you share the correct content, can boost your company's profile, create the impression that your company is a trusted source of information, and increase the traffic to your site. This can be content from journals, blogs, or even articles. Always start with a paragraph about why your company believes this content to be relevant and the key takeaways your reader can take from it. Then, copy the original content and reference the original source.

- **Four of your own posts:** This can include videos, articles, and other visuals on any topic related to your company, the industry you're in, and what your readers will be interested in. Since you'll have more time to compile these posts, you can genuinely wow your reader with your content.

- **One call to action:** Get your reader to interact with the company by asking them to do something. This can be doing an online poll, downloading something, buying your product, adding their email addresses to gain more information, or participating in a competition.

Since these calls to action won't be a daily occurrence, your reader won't necessarily see them as a sales pitch and will be more likely to act.

Handy Resources

The checklist is one of the most high-powered productivity tools ever discovered. –Brian Tracy

In this chapter, you will find

- a checklist of the eight simple business writing tips.
- suggestions for popular online tools you can use to improve your writing.
- a list of simpler word choices to use.
- common spelling mistakes to avoid.
- a guide to help you avoid confusing words.

It's easy to become so involved in your writing that you forget the basic tips discussed. For this reason, I've included a handy checklist of the eight simple tips you can quickly reference. You'll also find suggestions for online tools to help improve your writing, a guide on simpler word choices, common spelling mistakes to avoid, and commonly confused words that might sound the same but have vastly different meanings.

Checklist: 8 Simple Business Writing Tips

We've discussed these tips in great detail. If you ever feel unsure of how you should apply them, refer to the specific chapter for a refresher. This checklist is purely a reminder of what you should make sure to do before, during, and after your writing.

1. Define your purpose: Do I know why I'm writing and what outcome I'm trying to achieve?
2. Know your reader: Do I know who my reader is and how they prefer to be communicated with?
3. Organize your messages: Have I organized and structured my messages logically, and do I have answers for all the questions my reader might ask?
4. Use plain language: Am I using plain language that my reader will easily understand?
5. Make your writing inclusive and accessible: Does my writing include all my readers? Can all my readers access it?
6. Get the basics right: Am I making sure that I get at least the basics right when it comes to spelling, grammar, and punctuation?
7. Format your content for maximum readability: Am I formatting my content in a way that will make it as easy as possible for my reader to read and digest?
8. Edit your writing: Am I editing my content properly to try to fix all the mistakes I may have made?

Online Tools

With most of us sitting at our computers to do business writing, it's helpful to know the different online tools available at your fingertips to help improve your business writing. Listed below are some of the most popular tools you can use.

Writing assistance tools

- **Grammarly.** Grammarly can help improve the grammar, spelling, and punctuation of your writing. The basic version is available for free from **grammarly.com**. You can unlock more features if you upgrade to Grammarly Premium. For example, it can suggest rephrasing sentences for greater clarity, offer alternate words, identify repetition, and tell you if you're using passive language.

- **ProWritingAid.** ProWritingAid is a tool that can help you improve your writing by identifying grammar, style, and other issues in your text. It provides a variety of features, such as grammar checking, style analysis, and readability analysis. You can access the basic version for free from **prowritingaid.com** or pay a fee for premium features.

- **Thesaurus.** If you need to find synonyms for words and phrases to avoid repetition and add variety to your writing, a free online thesaurus is an excellent tool. Visit **thesaurus.com**.

- **Microsoft Editor.** Microsoft Editor is built into Microsoft Word and Outlook and is designed to help you improve the grammar, style, and tone of your written documents, emails, web pages, and social media content. Available in 20 languages.

- **Language Tool.** An open-source grammar, spelling, and style checker that supports more than 30 languages. Visit **languagetool.org**.

As helpful as these tools can be, their suggestions may not always be correct or suitable for your reader or industry, so take care when using them and use your judgment.

ChatGPT by OpenAI

One of the more recent developments in business writing is the use of artificial intelligence (AI). In November 2022, OpenAI made its powerful language model, ChatGPT, free to consumers. Trained on huge language sets and using machine learning, it can generate human-like text in response to prompts. Here are some ways you could use it to enhance your business writing:

- **Rephrasing.** You may have written your document following the tips in the book but want to explore different ways to phrase certain sentences or paragraphs. In this case, you could paste your text into the tool's prompt and request it to rephrase it.

- **Summarizing.** If you've written a document but think it's too long, you could use ChatGPT to reduce the word count. To do this, you would provide a prompt such as "rephrase this text to have a word count of 500" and then add your written text to the prompt. The output may not be perfect, but it could be a useful starting point for revising your content to be more concise.
- **Research.** In addition to providing instructional prompts, you can also pose questions to ChatGPT. This can help with your research by saving you time that would have been spent asking similar questions on a search engine and sifting through numerous results to find the information you require. Before you start, type in the prompt, "How current is your data?"to find out when the data was last updated.
- **Idea generation.** Have you ever known what you wanted to say but couldn't find the right words? For example, let's say you need to write a report to promote a new brand of sparkling water, and you want some headline suggestions. I tested ChatGPT by providing the prompt "Three headline options to promote a new brand of sparkling water." Here is the response it generated:

    1. Introducing the newest addition to your drink collection: XYZ Sparkling Water.
    2. Refresh your taste buds with XYZ Sparkling Water - now available!
    3. Get a taste of luxury with XYZ Sparkling Water - the ultimate refreshment.

At first glance, the response may seem pretty good. However, it's important to take into account your specific needs and your audience. For example, if your target audience is school students, using the word "luxury" in the headline may not be appropriate. I also couldn't help but notice the incorrect use of hyphens. Always remember to make sure you review the responses carefully and use your discretion.

The integration of AI in business writing is an exciting development, but it's important to remember that ChatGPT is simply another tool at your disposal. While helpful in rephrasing, summarizing, researching, and generating ideas, there is no substitute for you. It hasn't done your research, doesn't know the nuances of your audience, and can lack the creativity and uniqueness that human writers like you can bring.

If you're interested in trying ChatGPT for yourself, you can sign up for a free ChatGPT account at **beta.openai.com/signup**.

Accessibility tools

In Tip 5, we discussed how to make your documents accessible to more readers, particularly those who use assistive technology. If you use Microsoft Word, Excel, Outlook, or PowerPoint and are interested in learning more about the accessibility features of these programs, you can find a library of helpful training videos and user guides on the Microsoft website at **microsoft.com/accessibility**.

Simpler Word Choices

You should always look for the simplest way to convey your message. As discussed, doing this will make sure that your reader understands your message and can absorb it quicker than when you try to sound important or fancy using words your reader might not understand. Let's look at ways to use simpler word choices.

Don't use	**Use**
a sufficient number of	enough
accorded	given
accrue	increase
addressees	you
adjacent to	next to
adversely impact on	hurt, damage, or set back
afford an opportunity	allow or let
appreciable	many
approximate	about
as a means of	to
ascertain	find out or learn
at the present time	now
by means of	by or with
caveat	warning
close proximity	near
commence	begin or start
comply with	follow
component	part

comprise	include or make up
consolidate	combine, join, or merge
constitutes	is, forms, makes up
convene	meet
deem	believe, consider, or think
designate	appoint, choose, or name
disseminate	give, issue, pass, or send
due to the fact that	due to or since
effect modifications	make changes
encounter	meet
endeavor	try
enumerate	count
expedite	hasten or speed up
facilitate	ease or help
feasible	can be done or workable
forfeit	give up or lose
function	act, role, or work
furnish	give or send
has a requirement for	needs
herein	here
heretofore	until now
herewith	here or below
in accordance with	by, following, per, or under
in addition	also, besides, too
in an effort to	to

inasmuch as	since
incumbent upon	must
in lieu of	instead
in order to	to
in regard to	about, concerning, or on
in relation to	about, with, or to
interpose no objection	don't object
in the amount of	for
in the event of	if
in the near future	shortly or soon
in view of	since
is able to	can
is applicable to	applies to
is in consonance with	agrees with or follows
magnitude	size
methodology	method
necessitate	cause or need
notify	let know or tell
notwithstanding	in spite of or still
on a monthly basis	monthly
on the ground that	because
optimum	best, greatest, or most
parameters	limits
pertaining to	about, of, or on
portion	part

possess	have or own
practicable	practical
preclude	prevent
proficiency	skill
promulgate	issue or publish
provided that	if
provides guidance	guides
pursuant to	by, following, per, or under
reach out	contact, email, or call
relative to	about or on
remuneration	pay or payment
render	give or make
reside	live
retain	keep
set forth in	in
solicit	ask for or request
subsequent	later or next
the undersigned	I
transmit	send
under the provisions of	under
until such time as	until
utilize or utilization	use
with reference to	about
with the exception of	except for

Double Negatives

People often use double negatives to get their point across. Unfortunately, these double negatives don't add to your message. Instead, they waste the reader's time. Let's look at some examples to avoid in your writing.

Don't use	**Use**
due and payable	due
cease and desist	stop
knowledge and information	use either one of these, but not both
begin and commence	start

Common Spelling Mistakes

Spelling mistakes are often made in all forms of writing. They can easily be avoided by using automatic spell checkers in most word processing programs or checking the spelling in the dictionary. Let's look at words that are often misspelled.

Correct spelling	**How to remember it**
accommodate	There are four people living in the accommodation, two "cc" and two "mm."
acquire	People often forget to add the "c." Always remember that you can "c" what you acquire.
apparent	To remember how to write it, remember there is an "app" to make you a better "parent."

calendar	This word ends with an “ar,” the same as the month of March. Remember it by saying M*ar*ch is a month on the calendar.
colleague	You’ll be in a different *league* if you can spell *colleague*.
conscientious	If you’re conscientious, you shouldn’t just dot your “i’s” but also cross your “t’s.”
entrepreneur	An easy way to remember is that all the syllables have an “r” in them, except for the first one. One way to remember this is by using this phrase: The entrepreneur skipped the first syllable but wanted an “r” in each of the others.
experience	This is often spelled as “experiance.” Remember there should be an “e” in each syllable in experience.
fulfill	It’s first just one “l,” and then you use two “l’s.”
liaison	Two “i’s” are liaising with “a.”
license	“C” got their drivers’ license and is driving “s” around.
maintenance	Remember, the word “ten” is in it. “You have to do it ten times for proper maintenance.
necessary	A double “ss” makes it necessary.

privilege	Many people misspell this word and will write "priviledge." But you're so privileged that you don't need a "d."
recommend	This word combines the prefix "re" with "commend."
separate	The "r" separates two "a's."
stationery	This refers to the equipment you use when writing by hand, such as pens, pencils, and staplers. You can remember the spelling of this word by "e," which stands for envelope.

Commonly Confused Words

There are many different words that are commonly confused. These are often words that sound the same but have different meanings and spellings. One of the most common set of words is the following:

- **They're.** This is used to combine the words "they" and "are."
- **Their.** This refers to possession; for example, it's their research.
- **There.** This refers to a place; for example, the office is over there.

Another mistake many people make is with the words *to*, *too*, and *two*:

- **To.** This word is used to show time, place, and direction or to introduce something; for example, "I will go to her" or "I will wait to see."
- **Too.** This word can mean *also* or refer to something being excessive; for example, "I will go too" or "I have too much work."
- **Two.** This refers to the number two.

Let's look at some other words that are often confused.

you're This is the conjunction for *you are.*	**your** This refers to possession; for example, it's your pen.
it's This is a conjunction for *it is.*	**its** This is another possessive pronoun, such as their and your.
I This refers to myself.	**eye** This is the organ that you see with.
here This refers to where you are situated.	**hear** You use your ears to hear.
break If you're going on vacation, you're taking a break.	**brake** You press the brakes in the car to stop.
flower This grows outside in the garden.	**flour** You use this to make a cake.
our This refers to possession; for example, My team finished our research.	**hour** This refers to time.

Many people also use the words *can*, *may*, and *will* incorrectly:

- **Can.** This refers to physical ability. For example, when you ask, "Can I ride with you?" you're asking the person if they are physically capable of giving you a ride.

- **May.** This asks permission. For example, if you say, "May I ride with you?" you're asking permission to get a lift.

- **Will.** This is used to refer to something that will definitely happen. For example, "Will I ride with you?" you're asking if it is guaranteed that the person will give you a lift.

Conclusion

Good writing is good conversation, only more so.
–Ernest Hemingway

Effective writing is an essential skill for success in business. With the rise of remote working and digital communication, written content is a primary means of conveying information and making an impact. Writing with purpose, clarity, and confidence has never been more important.

As you've been reading this book, I hope you've started to put into practice the tips you've learned. There's no time like the present to start honing your skills and delivering quality content that is simple and easy for your reader to understand.

Always remember to start with your purpose and clarify your reader's needs. Define and organize your messages so they flow and make logical sense. Use plain language and ensure your writing is inclusive and accessible to a wide range of readers. Check that your work is error-free, format it thoughtfully, and edit it carefully. Finally, use the templates, tools, and resources referenced in this book to make your document as good as it can be.

If you do this, you'll be well on your way to communicating better at work. You'll increase your productivity by reducing the time spent editing and rewriting and gain influence as your readers recognize the value you can deliver.

If you find the writing process overwhelming at any point, refer back to the eight simple tips discussed in this book. Keep in mind that the more you write, the easier it will become. Just stick to it. You can do it!

If you enjoyed the book and think *8 Simple Business Writing Tips* can help more people achieve success in their writing, please leave a review on Amazon.

About the Author

For over 25 years, James Dare has been helping individuals, businesses, and brands tell their stories. He's worked with small startups, large multinationals, and government agencies, crafting clear, concise, and compelling messages that deliver business outcomes.

Over the years, his approach to business communication has remained steadfast: Simplicity is key. Today, more than ever, the ability to communicate clearly and concisely is essential to business success.

In *8 Simple Business Writing Tips*, James shares his eight tips to help anyone who wants to improve their business writing—from someone starting their career to professionals looking to update their skills. He provides insight into what makes good business writing and practical guidance on how to do it.

References

Ammanath, B ., & Firth-Butterfield, K. (2021, November 11). *Chatbots and other virtual assistants are here to stay – here's what that means. World Economic Forum.* https://www.weforum.org/agenda/2021/11/chatbots-and-other-virtual-assistants-are-here-to-stay-for-good-or-bad/

An introduction to NLP and its importance in today's technology landscape (2023, 10 January), AITopics. https://aitopics.org/doc/news:75334AA8

Benton, D. (2021, July 20). *The power of reader-centered business writing.* Debra Benton. https://www.debrabenton.com/blog/reader-centered-business-writing/

Bernoff, J. (2016, September 6). *New research on business writing (infographic and report).* Without Bullshit. https://withoutbullshit.com/blog/new-research- on-business-writing-infographic-and-report

Brockway, L. H. (2015, July 23). *13 clever and inspiring quotes about writing.* Entrepreneur. https://www.entrepreneur.com/business-news/13-clever-and- inspiring-quotes-about-writing/248467

Building accessible Tables. (n.d). Dallas College. https://www.dallascollege.edu/about/accessibility/guidelines/pages/building-tables.aspx

Business Writing. (25 C.E., October). Corporate Finance Institute. https://corporate financeinstitute.com/resources/career/business-writing/

Chesson, D. (2023, January 3). *Grammarly Review [2023 Update]: Is Grammarly Worth It?* Kindlepreneur. https://kindlepreneur.com/grammarly-review-is-grammarly-good/

Chesson, D. (2023, January 3). *ProWritingAid Review [2023]: Is It Worth it?* Kindlepreneur. https://kindlepreneur.com/prowritingaid-review/

Choudary, A. (n.d.). *Effective written communication: Introduction and when and when not to use written communication.* Pharmaguideline. https://www.pharmaguideline.com/2021/10/effective-written-communication.html

Communicating chemistry: A framework for sharing science. (n.d.). https://nap.nationalacademies.org/read/23444/chapter/5

Creating accessible tables. (n.d). Microsoft. https://support.microsoft.com/en-us/office/video-create-accessible-tables-in-word-cb464015-59dc-46a0-ac01-6217c62210e5

Cruthers, A. (n.d.). *Using inclusive language.* Kpu.pressbooks.pub. https://kpu.pressbooks.pub/hrcommunication/chapter/using-inclusive-language/

Duke, C. (n.d.). *The cost of bad writing in business.* PomoDoneApp. https://pomodoneapp.com/blog.html/2019/11/20/the-cost-of-bad-writing-in-business-and-how-to-deal-with-it/

Add alternative text to a shape, picture, chart, SmartArt graphic, or other object. (n.d). Microsoft. https://support.microsoft.com/en-us/office/add-alternative-text-to-a-shape-picture-chart-smartart-graphic-or-other-object-44989b2a-903c-4d9a-b742-6a75b451c669#PickTab=Windows

Famous quotes on writing. (2020, July 10). The Writers College Times. https://www.writerscollegeblog.com/famous-quotes-on-writing/

Ferron, E. (2017, February 16). *Mobile 101: What are bots, chatbots and virtual assistants?* New Atlas. https://newatlas.com/what-is-bot-chatbot-guide/47965/

Five quotes to improve your writing at work. (2013, July 30). Better Writing Tips. http://www.better-writing-tips.com/5-quotes-to-improve-your-writing-at-work/

Formats for different business letter types. (n.d.). Universal Class. https://www.universalclass.com/articles/writing/business-writing/formats-for-different-business-letters.htm

Formatting business writing. (n.d.). Lumen. https://courses.lumenlearning.com/ wm-businesscommunicationmgrs/chapter/formatting-business-writing/

Forsey, C. (2022, June 21). *How to use and promote inclusive language at your organization.* Hubspot. https://blog.hubspot.com/marketing/inclusive-language

Gormandy White, M. (n.d.). *Fundamental spelling rules for everyone to know.* Your Dictionary. https://grammar.yourdictionary.com/spelling-and-word-lists/ spelling-rules.html

Grammarly. (2022, September 23). *5 spelling rules to know.* https://www.grammarly.com/blog/spelling/

Guinness, H. (2020, April 7). *How to edit your own writing.* The New York Times. https://www.nytimes.com/2020/04/07/smarter-living/how-to-edit-your-own-writing.html

Gunner, J. (2018, March 23). *The basic grammar rules of English.* Your Dictionary. https://grammar.yourdictionary.com/grammar-rules-and-tips/basic-english-grammar-rules.html

Herrity, J. (2022, June 28). *How to write a meeting agenda: Tips, template and sample.* Indeed Career Guide. https://www.indeed.com/career-advice/ career-development/how-to-write-a-meeting-agenda

How does a chatbot work? (n.d) Drift. https://www.drift.com/learn/chatbot/how-does-a-chatbot-work/

I*nsights discovery & color types: A beginners guide.* (2016, January 27). The Colour Works. https://www.thecolourworks.com/insights-discovery-colour-types-guide

Instantly Enhance Your Writing. (n.d), Language Tool. https://languagetool.org/

Johnson, A. (2022, Dec 7) *Here's What To Know About OpenAI's ChatGPT—What It's Disrupting And How To Use It.* Forbes. https://www.forbes.com/sites/ariannajohnson/2022/12/07/heres-what-to-know-about-openais-chatgpt-what-its-disrupting-and-how-to-use-it/?sh=79d835e52643

Johnson, A., & Jones, C. (2022, September 22). *Content relevance and usefulness: Why you need it and four ways to achieve it.* Content Science Review. https://review.content-science.com/content-relevance-and-usefulness-why-you-need-it-and-4-ways-to-achieve-it/

Justesen, I. (2017, October 11). *11 tips for editing your own writing.* Constant Content. https://www.constant-content.com/content-writing-service/2017/10/11-tips-for-editing-your-own-writing/

Kawarsky, D. (2022, February 25). *Why companies should invest in a business writing skills workshop?* The Soft Skills Group. https://www.tssg.ca/offering- business-writing-training-to-your-employees/

Know your audience. (n.d.). Skills You Need. https://www.skillsyouneed.com/write/ know-your-audience.html

Lanouette, J. (2012, December 24). *A history of three-act structure.* Screentakes. https://www.screentakes.com/an-evolutionary-study-of-the-three-act-structure- model-in-drama/

Make your Word documents accessible to people with disabilities. (n.d.). Microsoft. https://support.microsoft.com/en-us/office/make-your-word-documents-accessible-to-people-with-disabilities

McLeod, D. (2016, March 9). *En dash vs. em dash vs. hyphen - How to properly use them.* Grammarist. https://grammarist.com/usage/hyphen-en-dash-or-em-dash

Merriam-Webster. (n.d.). *Definition of powwow.* https://www.merriam-webster.com/ dictionary/powwow

Microsoft Editor checks grammar and more in documents, mail, and the web. (n.d) Microsoft. https://support.microsoft.com/en-us/office/microsoft-editor-checks-grammar-and-more-in-documents-mail-and-the-web-91ecbe1b-d021-4e9e-a82e-abc4cd7163d7

Minto, B M (2009, January 13). *The Pyramid Principle: Logic in Writing and Thinking,* 3rd Edition. Financial Times/Prentice Hall

Nordquist, R. (2020, February 4). *Best practices for business writing.* ThoughtCo. https://www.thoughtco.com/what-is-business-writing-1689188

Organizing information for business writing. (n.d.). Scribendi. https://www.scribendi. com/academy/articles/organizing_information_for_business_writing.en.html

ChatGPT: Optimizing Language Models for Dialogue. (n.d). Open AI. https://openai.com/blog/chatgpt/.

Paquet, M. (2021, April 6). *12 tips for creating the best email subject lines.* Constant Contact. https://www.constantcontact.com/blog/good-email-subject-lines/

Requesting feedback on writing. (n.d.). The Writing Center. https://writingcenter.unc.edu/esl/resources/requesting-feedback-on-writing/

Salter, M. (n.d.). *10 examples of bad grammar to avoid.* Your Dictionary. https://examples.yourdictionary.com/bad-grammar-examples.html

Schmidt, E. (2022, March 16). *Reading the numbers: 130 million American adults have low literacy skills.* APM Research Lab. https://www.apmresearchlab.org/ 10x-adult-literacy

6 steps that will help you organize your thoughts before writing. (2021, June 10). Think Marketing. https://thinkmarketingmagazine.com/6-steps-that-will-help- you-organize-your-thoughts-before-writing/

Smith, J. (2019). *Unit 4: Knowing your purpose for writing.* Kpu.pressbooks.pub. https://kpu.pressbooks.pub/communicationsatwork/chapter/2-1-knowing-your-purpose-for-writing/

Society for Neuroscience. (n.d.). *Dyslexia: What brain research reveals about reading.* LD Online. https://www.ldonline.org/ld-topics/reading-dyslexia/dyslexia-what- brain-research-reveals-about-reading

Spencer, L. (2022). *5 reasons your writing is misunderstood.* Writing Thoughts. https://www.writingthoughts.com/5-reasons-your-writing-is-misunderstood/

Sperry, I. (2016, October 11). *10 tips for writing effective business emails.* Firsthand. https://firsthand.co/blogs/networking/10-tips-for-writing-effective-business-emails

Spors, K. (2022, August 24). *Business letter formats.* Small Biz Ahead. https://sba.thehartford.com/business-management/marketing/business-letter-formats/

Sulmonte, A. (2021, January 31). *7 steps to communicate and achieve expected outcomes.* Anthony Sulmonte Redefining Leadership. https://asulmonte.com/7-steps-communicate-achieve-expected-outcomes-leadership/

33 accessibility statistics you need to know in 2022. (November 16, 2022). Monsido. https://monsido.com/blog/accessibility-statistics

Thompson, S. (2015, February 19). *5 super simple ways to show your readers you understand them.* KoMarketing: B2B Search, Social, & Content Marketing. https://komarketing.com/blog/understand-your-readers/

Top 9 strategies for writing an effective business email. (2017, May 11). Salesforce. https://www.salesforce.com/blog/strategies-writing-effective-business-email-blog/

Top 21 business writing quotes. (n.d.). A-Z Quotes. https://www.azquotes.com/quotes/topics/business-writing.html

Twelve inspiring quotes about writing to communicate. (2016, June 28). Writers Write. https://www.writerswrite.co.za/12-inspiring-quotes-about-writing-to-communicate/

Use simple words and phrases. (n.d.). Plain Language. https://www.plainlanguage.gov/guidelines/words/use-simple-words-phrases/

Write and learn with us. (nd.) ProWritingAid. https://prowritingaid.com/

Wylie, A. (2016, December 26). *Quotes on conversational business writing.* Wylie Communications, Inc. https://www.wyliecomm.com/2016/12/quotes-on- conversational-writing/

Notes

NOTES

NOTES

Made in the USA
Monee, IL
11 June 2025